D1081701

THE 2012 BID

FIVE CITIES CHASING THE SUMMER GAMES

by
Chetan Davé

authorHOUSE™

1663 LIBERTY DRIVE, SUITE 200
BLOOMINGTON, INDIANA 47403
(800) 839-8640
WWW.AUTHORHOUSE.COM

First published by AuthorHouse 06/21/05

ISBN: 1-4208-6227-8 (sc)

Printed in the United States of America
Bloomington, Indiana

This book is printed on acid-free paper.

This book is in no way affiliated with or endorsed by the International Olympic Committee (IOC) or any of the National Olympic Committees or bid committees. This book has been written using information that is freely available in the public domain. The writing of the words "Olympic", "Olympics", and "Olympic Games" has been used for editorial purposes only and is not intended to suggest any connection with the IOC or any other organization.

Novels by Chetan Davé:

Datoga Island

Bronx Cheer

For more information:

www.chetandave.com

or

www.ultimatewriter.com

For Her.

In recognition of all of the volunteers and professionals who have served on organizing or bid committees throughout the history of the Games.

TABLE OF CONTENTS

The race to secure the bid for the Summer Olympics and Paralympics of 2012 is among the most intense in history. Five of the world's most prominent cities have tossed their hat into the ring for the right to host the most prestigious international event in sports. They have consciously chosen to saddle the immense responsibility that comes with a winning bid. It seems that, more than any impending Olympics, the 2012 bid has garnered substantial media and public attention and scrutiny well before the host city was due to be decided. Never before has the competition been so close and packed with an almost tangible tension. The five cities to make it to the final round have gone to tremendous lengths to prove to the world and, more importantly, to the International Olympic Committee (IOC) that their bid is the most worthy. Madrid, Moscow, Paris, London, and New York are battling it out in this battle of metropolises to see who will be the last city standing in this global political, civic, athletic, and financial battle of pride to be known as the 2012 host city.

The first modern Olympic Games, held in 1896, were awarded during the IOC's first Session, which took place in Paris from the 18th to the 23rd of June in 1894, to the city of Athens, who faced no competition as there were no other candidate cities. The French Capital got its turn four years later. Paris was given the first Summer Games of the twentieth century (1900) uncontested. The first duel to secure Olympic hosting rights occurred between two American cities. St. Louis was awarded the Games in 1904 after being in contention with Chicago. The number of candidate cities would temporarily grow from there. The year 1908 saw the first multi-city selection process where London was awarded the Games in favor of Milan, Berlin, and the original winner of the bid, Rome, who relinquished hosting rights to the British Capital due to financial reasons. The one horse race for hosting rights had been eliminated… for the most part. Since 1908, only Stockholm in 1912 and Los Angeles in 1932 and 1984 have escaped the ultimate process for winning the Summer Games by not having to face off against another contending city for a final IOC vote during the concluding round of host city selection known as the candidature process. Chamonix (France) in 1924 and

Lake Placid (USA) in 1980 shared similar good fortunes on the Winter Olympics side.

Sports enthusiasts the world over, take pride in rattling off the Olympic years and locations: Mexico City 1968, Albertville 1992, Berlin 1936. But we may never precisely know how much time and effort the organizing committees spent in the hectic years of planning and construction between winning the right to host the Games and actually staging the Olympics. What were the issues facing Sapporo (Japan) organizers in 1969, three years before they would have to deliver the Winter Olympics? What was being discussed at organizing committee meetings in Helsinki in 1951, the year before their Summer Games? Taking that a step further, it is highly unlikely that we will ever be able to estimate similar information for those who served on bid committees of cities that never got selected to host the Games. What was the mood amongst the Buenos Aires bid committee on the night of April 27,1949 at their hotel in Rome, not knowing that within 24 hours, they would lose out on the 1956 Summer Games to Melbourne by a single vote in the deciding fourth round following three rounds of inconclusive balloting? What ran through the minds of the members of the Philadelphia bid committee as they watched the first mass televised Games take place in London in

1948, instead of being able to show the world the city they called home?

Four cities will face similar questions for the rest of their lives starting this year. Conversely, the seven-year fate of the winning city's future will be decided this summer. No one will know how this race ends until the 6th of July 2005 in Singapore when the fortunate winning city will emerge from the 117th Session of the IOC. Each contestant possesses unique historical and contemporary qualities to offer the sporting world. They are five different cities that may as well be five different worlds. They have meticulously planned and tirelessly showcased their proposals for years on end. But only one city will stand supreme. And four others will be left to pick up the pieces. Whatever the outcome, none of the candidate city bid committees have given a less than maximal effort to secure the 2012 bid.

In listening to the candidate city organizers and reading their detailed reports, one gets the impression that there very possibly could be five different Olympics taking place in the summer of 2012. Very often, we only tune in to the Games as they are happening and are not aware of the behemoth of background and planning work that goes into hosting this grand competition. Headlines are available to us on a daily basis. But going behind them, to cold, hard numbers reveals the total, mind-boggling span of logistics and resources required by a city's organizing committee to even be considered for hosting an Olympic Games. This is the story of what each city has to offer and how they plan on going about making the 2012 Summer Games a reality. This book aims to condense what is a mountain of numbers and documents diligently presented by each candidate city into information that is slightly simpler to understand for outsiders to give the reader a clearer view into the rather exclusive and often unforgiving world of planning to host the Olympics.

It is important to note that the cities bidding for the Games were instructed explicitly by the IOC to keep their focus during planning squarely on the athletes and to deliver a compact and cost efficient Games. All numerical projections and financial estimates are based on figures generated by the respective organizing committees that are subject to change. Monetary figures are presented in the currency of United States Dollars.

HOW THEY GOT HERE

On Tuesday January 21, 2003 Madrid beat out Seville by a vote of 157 to 103 among delegates of Spain's Olympic Committee for the right to become the country's candidate city to bid for the 2012 Olympics. It was the first of many necessary victories in the extended selection process on the way to 2012. The organizers had inched closer to the long-standing dream of making Madrid an Olympic city. Their focus would now turn to the international bidding that lay ahead.

It was not the city's first try at landing the Games. Madrid's only previous attempt at this dream came in 1972 when it lost out to Munich by a vote of 31 to 16 and the Spanish capital had to settle for hosting the World Weightlifting Championships a year later. Detroit and Montreal had also been unsuccessful in securing the '72

7

bid. But neither of those cities came as close as Madrid. Of the three unsuccessful candidates that year, only Montreal was rewarded with the Summer Games four years later. Madrid and Detroit are still on the outside looking in.

Barcelona successfully won the bid for and hosted the 1992 Summer Olympics. Who could forget the archer's flaming arrow lighting the cauldron at Montjuic Olympic Stadium to open the festivities? Since then the only other Spanish bid city had been Seville, which lost out in the bidding for the 2008 Summer Games to Beijing. This time around it is Madrid's turn. The metropolis with the long sports history and one of the most successful football (soccer) teams in the world in Real Madrid as well as one of the most prominent basketball teams of the same name in all of Europe still lacks the title of Olympic City. Organizers are hoping that they can make the jump to the top on this try.

Among the five cities in contention, Moscow can boast of most recently having hosted an Olympic Games, after successfully staging the 1980 Summer Olympics. This gives the organizers increased credibility as they are only 25 years removed from holding the event. Granted, those Games were boycotted by a number of nations for political reasons, but the event as a whole went off without incident with the 5000 plus athletes from the 80 nations who participated. Six years before 1980, Moscow had squared off with an American city. That bid had won by an IOC vote in Vienna on October 13, 1974 where Moscow beat out Los Angeles by a count of 39 to 20. Another little known fact taking place on this date is nice gem for sports historians. Given the geopolitical situation of the time, it was ironic that, on the very same day that Moscow got the Summer Games, Lake Placid was also awarded the 1980 Winter Games without competition from any other city. Some would like to call it the 'Miracle on Ballots'.

So the second time proved to be the charm for Moscow. The city had previously lost out on the 1976 Summer Olympics to Montreal by a vote of 41 to 28 at an IOC Session in Amsterdam on May 12, 1970.

The city of Paris has claim to a rich, modern Olympic history. It is one of the few cities associated with the Olympic movement from its very inception. The French capital has hosted the Summer Games in 1900 and 1924. The first bid was the easy one. For the 1900 Games, there were no other candidate cities in the running. But it wasn't an exclusive event similar to what we see today. These Games were held as a part of the Paris World's Fair and the events were spread out over five months time. Do you think the networks would block out that kind of time today? This was also the first time women participated in the Modern era of the Games. Due to the length of the event leading to a decreased importance placed on the Games, some athletes died without ever knowing they had even participated in the Olympics. The 1924 bid was a bit more challenging with the city having to beat out Amsterdam, Los Angeles, Barcelona, Prague, and Rome for hosting rights. A few of the traditions we see today were born during these Games. The Olympic motto was introduced here as well as the custom of raising the flags of the IOC, current host nation, and subsequent host nation during the closing ceremonies. The 1924 Games also saw an increased interest in the Olympic concept worldwide. The participation of 44 nations, compared to the previous Games' total of 29 in Antwerp in 1920, signified a sharp increase in the international recognition of the Games as the premier global sporting event.

The city has a recent history of bidding for the Summer Games as well. Paris finished second in the voting for the 1992 Games and third in the balloting for the 2008 Games.

The country has fared slightly better on the Winter Olympic side. France has hosted three other Winter Games. The first time, it turned out, was a great sports year for the nation. Chamonix was chosen to host in 1924 as the site later classified as the first ever Winter Olympics because the country hosting the Summer Games for that year had first right to hold the Winter Games as well. Over four decades later, France hit winter pay dirt again. Grenoble won the bid for 1968 on January 28, 1964 at an IOC vote in Innsbruck, Austria. Other contending cities were Calgary, Sapporo, Lake Placid, Oslo, and Lahti (Finland). But it didn't come easy. The winning of the bid required three tense rounds of voting. In the first round Grenoble, Calgary, and Lahti garnered 15, 12, and 11 votes, respectively, leaving the other three cities behind and advancing to round two. In the next round, Grenoble's 18 votes were fewer than Calgary's 19 and enough to eliminate Lahti with its 14 votes. In the final and deciding round, Grenoble edged out Calgary 27 to 24 to finally secure the bid. It was eighteen years before they jumped into the snow again. France's nail biting election history continued on October 16, 1986 in Lausanne, Switzerland where Albertville outlasted a staggering six rounds of IOC voting along with Sofia, Falun (Sweden), Lillehammer, Cortina d'Empezzo (Italy), Anchorage (USA), and Berchtesgaden (West Germany) to earn the 1992 Winter Games. This time, the voting frequency was even deeper. In the sixth round, Albertville decisively won the vote over Sofia by a margin of 51 to 25 with Falun finishing with 9 votes. It seems France has way of pulling these things out. The 1992 Albertville Games were the last to be held in the same year with the Summer Games.

The British Capital has an interesting Olympic hosting history. Even though it has hosted the Summer Olympics twice before, in 1908 and 1948, the city of London has never hosted after winning an Olympic bid. The 1908 Summer Games were won by Rome, but, for financial reasons following a volcano, the Italian capital was forced to relinquish hosting rights, which were then allocated to London. It was four decades before the Games returned there. The 1948 Games, the first ever to be shown on domestic television, were awarded to London on short notice because London had originally won the bid for the 1944 Games that were canceled due to World War II. Five other challengers went home empty handed for 1948. America lost out on the 1948 Games after having Baltimore,

Minneapolis, Philadelphia, and Los Angeles as candidate cities along with Lausanne, Switzerland.

At certain times, historic ideas can come from unexpected places. London and England can take credit for helping inspire IOC founder Baron Pierre de Coubertin to plan the Modern Olympics. It happened near the end of the 19th century on a trip to a sleepy British county. After visiting the traditional Olympian Society Annual Games in 1890 in the Shropshire town of Much Wenlock, complete with pre-event ceremonies comprised of flag bearers, athletes, and officials, de Coubertin returned to France and penned an article in a local paper about an idea for an Olympic rebirth. He decided the best and most historically appropriate place to start would be in Greece.

On November 2, 2002 the USOC named New York City as the USA's representative to bid for the 2012 Olympics ending the two horse race between New York and San Francisco. Prior to that Cincinnati, Dallas, Los Angeles, Washington D.C., and Tampa had been eliminated from contention in previous months. New York City has never bid for the Olympic Games although numerous other American cities have successfully hosted the Summer (St. Louis in

1904, Los Angeles in 1932 and 1984, and Atlanta in 1996) and Winter (Lake Placid in 1932 and 1980, Squaw Valley in 1960, and Salt Lake City in 2002) Games. In the event of a winning bid, New York would become the city to host America's ninth Olympic Games.

The state of Missouri welcomed the first Olympics held in America. St. Louis received the bid for the 1904 Summer Games after Chicago, which originally had won, decided to pass it on to its neighbor to the south. These Games were lost in the shuffle of the adjacent World's Fair that same year. It would be nearly three decades before the Games returned to the States. Los Angeles was the only city competing for the 1932 Summer Games, which it hosted for second time in 1984 when the Soviet Union boycotted, again with no other candidate cities as contenders. If only every city should have such luck. Atlanta and Athens battled for five rounds of voting along with earlier round exits from Melbourne, Manchester, Toronto, and Belgrade before Atlanta won the 1996 bid by a vote of 51 to 35 on September 18, 1990 in Tokyo. For American cities, hosting the Winter Olympics has required competition at the beginning. Before hosting the 1932 Winter Games, Lake Placid (New York) won the bid over a then record 8 competing cities, which included Montreal and Oslo along with fellow American cities

Denver, Bear Mountain (New York), Duluth (Minnesota), Minneapolis, Lake Tahoe and Yosemite Valley (California). The second time proved much easier for the upstate New York town. Lake Placid received the 1980 Winter Olympic bid without contention. It was able to introduce a technological breakthrough that year as well. This marked the first time artificial ice was produced for an Olympic Games. The state of California entered the alpine fray midway through the twentieth century. Squaw Valley edged out Innsbruck (Austria) 32 to 30 in two rounds of voting to host the 1960 Winter Games. There was, however, a bit of controversy involved with the 1960 Games. This was the only Games that lacked a bobsled competition after organizers refused to build a bobsled track citing only nine nations had offered teams that would compete. What would the Olympics in California be without a little star power? Walt Disney presided over the opening and closing ceremonies. Most recently, the state of Utah successfully landed the Winter Games on June 16, 1995 in an IOC vote in Belgrade. Salt Lake City needed only one round of voting to decisively wrap up the 2002 Winter Olympics emerging from a field that included Ostersund (Sweden), Sion (Switzerland), and Quebec City.

OVERTURE

Sometimes, the year of the event has a significant meaning behind it. It may not be a coincidence that the Spanish Olympic Committee is set to celebrate its centennial in 2012. It is not hard to guess that organizers would be thrilled to mark the milestone by hosting the Games themselves. But the seeds for this project were planted way back in 1997 with the introduction by the city government of the General Urban Development Plan with the primary objective of landing the 2012 Games. It was an important step going forward for the city. In that plan, the City outlined the reservation of 250 hectares of public land that was close in proximity to the Barajas International Airport, which would minimize the transportation gridlock issues typically faced by other host cities. They were also able to make use of little used areas of the town. The project aimed to revitalize two of the city's relatively undeveloped sectors, an old mining area on the city's east end and the southern waterfront along the Manzanares River. It would breathe new life into the area as well as provide some modern history with which to stand on. Following the Games, this space would result in civic parks, professional and amateur athletic facilities, and student dormitories.

The Russian Capital can point to successful past Olympic results to give anyone an idea of the nation's rich sporting history. Over 500 Olympic Champions call Moscow home and most of them are actively involved in supporting the bid for the 2012 Olympic and Paralympic Games. Organizers here also have a date with history should Moscow win the bid. The 100-year anniversary of Russia's first participation in the Olympic Games will take place in the year 2012. The city has a large plus point when it comes to the venues themselves. One of Moscow's greatest strengths is having much of the sports infrastructure, constructed for the 1980 Games, still standing and in use. This would appear to be an efficient advantage in terms of required expenditure. Citing the IOC's emphasis on controlling costs and providing sustainable facilities for public use, this gives the organizing committee tangible proof to present to the IOC that the local citizens gained valuable resources from the building and maintenance of those venues and continue to use them effectively even today for the promotion of sport throughout the city and country. This, in part, has allowed the nation to sustain the sporting excellence for which it is typically known. Most importantly in the IOC's eyes, it shows that the people of the country benefited from the event itself. Organizers have some convincing data to show this point. Currently, greater than 70% of the venues for the 1980 Games are used on a daily basis by athletes for competition as well as providing for ideal training facilities. This infrastructure is capable of being transitioned to the current era. The idea for 2012 is to use the foundation laid down for 1980 and modify, renovate, and convert the facilities to bring those structures into the 21st Century as modern and attractive sports venues. It would be a win-win situation. This way, the standards of the IOC are upheld and the local people would be left with contemporary athletic sites to continue to enjoy for years to come. A state of civic sporting similar to the post-1980 period could be seen as a hopeful outcome of the 2012 Games in Moscow. By winning the Games, organizers would like to reinforce the Olympic ideals and bring a large amount of pride to the people of the city and country.

The organizers in France always seem to deliver what the IOC is looking for. In pursuing the 2012 bid, Paris seeks to modernize itself and surrounding vicinity as well as refreshing the ideals that were once an integral part of French culture. The change has become necessary at this point in the city's history as the urban infrastructure has become somewhat dated. The Olympics would provide the city with the impetus to overhaul its urban planning practices, revitalize an aging public transport system, and create a host of sporting facilities still lacking in the metropolitan region. There is also hope that the Games would have some sort of sociologic effect. The organizing committee wishes to disperse Olympic values by welcoming the athletes to an Olympic village that is close by to their place of competition, placing the celebration of the history of the Olympics as a main objective for promotion throughout the Games, and involving as many sectors of the community as possible to reconstruct the civic and sporting infrastructure of Paris and the Ile-de-France region. If achieved, it could be an enjoyable transformation for everyone involved. The overall idea here is to somehow unite Parisians and motivate them to rebuild certain aspects of their city for the current and future good of themselves and others. The others would refer to the waves of people who visit the city annually to fuel the robust tourism industry.

A similar revitalization concept seems to be employed by organizers in Britain. London aims to resurrect underdeveloped areas of its city and provide its citizens with facilities and parks for use by future generations. There are a number of benefits expected to spawn as a result of the event. The organizing committee believes the awarding of the 2012 Games to London would create numerous jobs, new housing, and novel athletic facilities. The general public would also stand to gain from the post-Olympic landscape. The plans also include the establishment of one of the largest centrally located city parks in all of Europe. The Games would provide the country with another notch in its storied athletic past. London plans to build on the UK's rich sporting history which included the introduction of a number of sports that are played in the Olympics today as well as being the original creators of the Paralympics.

New York is the other newcomer in the group. Known as the land of opportunity, where people from all over the world come and build their lives alongside one another, New York plans to have the Olympics launch the city into a period of fraternity and development while hoping to show the world that the city can accommodate visitors as diverse as its citizens. Quite a bit of modernization would be required. Redevelopment of the city focuses on the site of the Olympic Village across the East River from the UN, the West Side of Manhattan, and a refurbishing of abandoned riverbanks into more environmentally friendly parkland. Organizers hope to translate a rich domestic sporting history into one that includes the largest international sporting event as well.

GENERAL GAMES PLAN

Spain's capital offers large portions of environmentally friendly land. Approximately 40% of the total area of Madrid is in the form of parks, which is why the locals like to call it the "green city". Bringing the Olympics to the city would probably increase that number. The Madrid plan consists of three primary areas of activity. Each of the "Sectors" as they are known would host their own collection of events. The East Sector would be developed to host sixteen events. The centerpiece of the sector would be the Olympic Park. The projected Olympic Park would be constructed on top of a former mineral quarry, which would be restored to pre-development capacity once the Games were finished. It would serve as the main location for welcoming the nations of the world to Madrid. This site would also contain the venue for the opening and closing ceremonies. The city's principal exposition center would also be incorporated as an Olympic venue. The 12 halls of Madrid's IFEMA trade fair grounds, which were opened in 1980 and renovated in 2002, would accommodate several sporting events as well as the Main Press Center (MPC) and International Broadcast Center (IBC). The center would provide a convenient staging area for the potential onslaught of media activity that would arrive in 2012. This facility normally reserved for business conventions and trade shows boasts ample parking and provides a variety of public transport options to its visitors. Local communities would also undertake hosting privileges. The municipalities of Paracuellos, Rivas Vaciamadrid, and Coslada would be used to host Olympic sporting events. The proximity to the city's aerial hub would assist in the success of this sector as the main host area. The majority of the Olympic events would be hosted here because this sector is located directly west of the Barajas Airport. The next sector is concentrated more towards central Madrid. The Central Axis is the equivalent of drawing a straight north-south line through the middle of Madrid. It's as if a cake has been sliced right in half. This area encompasses the city center where many historical and cultural sites can be found. This option would serve to attract a non-sporting audience as well. The southern end of this line, the projected South Park of the Manzanares River, is where the development of sports venues would occur. The final sector in question would accommodate mostly outdoor events. The West Sector, which is currently home to the city's many so-called green zones, provides an ideal area for hosting grass field events such as hockey, equestrian, and archery.

Public transport is highly stressed by organizers for use by the public as well as the Olympic Family. As the venues are mostly concentrated, Madrid claims it can pull off the first ever "car free" Olympics by utilizing its vast public transport system consisting of subways, suburban trains, and buses. Selected traffic provisions would be instituted in the event Madrid wins the bid. The city and organizing committee have set aside one lane in each of the city's four encompassing ring roads just for athletes and members of the extended Olympic Family. The proximity of sectors to one another should provide for decreased time of intra-city travel. The commuting times between any two venues is said to be less than 26 minutes for all of the Madrid city-based Olympic sites.

Moscow plans to incorporate its natural landscape into its Olympic campaign. Introducing its Olympic River concept, the Moscow River is at the core of the Russian Capital's bid project. This would provide for a scenic commute no matter the type of transport used. The majority of the venues would be located throughout 5 complexes along the Moscow River all within 10 km of one another and accessible by a variety of transportation modes including ferryboat service. The summertime vistas would prove to be aesthetically pleasing to visitors of all sorts.

Commuting distance is often a concern at an event of this scale. The committee promises short travel times between venues for athletes, delegates, and fans by the use of water taxis, which have around 70 passenger piers along the river from which to dock. This vista would prove beneficial for the media as well. From a broadcast standpoint, the background of the river should provide picturesque views and an aura of tranquility to beam to the television viewers of the world. The currently standing venues are an example of how the city was able to translate past Olympic success to civic benefits. Moscow intends to continue using most if not all of the new as well as the older enhanced facilities long after the end of the Games, a fact that has been put into practice for all to see since 1980.

The French intend to utilize the periphery of their capital to occupy the majority of the required facilities. The plan in Paris is to situate most of the venues along the circumference of the city's ring road, thereby leaving the center of town open for pedestrian celebration. Accommodation for the athletes would be the vertex of the strategy. The Olympic Village would be the centerpiece around which would be two groups of venues the organizing committee is calling "clusters" located north and west of Paris with both clusters being 6 km on either side of the Village. This way, the athletes would be housed equidistant from the majority of the venues.

According to organizers, accommodation for the rest of us would also be ample. The vast collection of hotels already available throughout Paris alleviates any concern of housing for non-athletes. There would also be dedicated road transport provisions provided for the Games. The roads leading to the venues would have marked so called "fast lanes" which would allow expedited travel for athletes and officials ensuring their prompt arrival for competition and training.

In England also, there is a plan for a principal park around which the project would revolve. Located in Stratford in east London, the Olympic Park would serve as the centerpiece of the British Capital's Games plan. City officials have cleared this area for use for the Olympics. The Park would be constructed on 600 hectares of reclaimed land and would include a network of canals that would serve the area for revitalization after the Games. The main communication and athlete accommodation hubs would be located in this compound. All media facilities, the athletes' village, selected temporary venues, the cycling velodrome, the aquatic center, hockey center, four multi sport arenas (for fencing, basketball, handball, and volleyball), as well as the Olympic Stadium would all be placed within the boundaries of the Park. The placement of the Village was selected for a reason. The housing for the athletes would be located no more than 15 minutes from over 50% of the venues and the center of town would be 5 to 7 minutes by train. The commuter system would be capable of handling the heavy loads of passengers normally associated with the Games. What organizers are calling the "Best-ever Games Transport" scheme would move up to 240,000 people per hour to the Olympic Park area by train, Underground (subway), bus, and park and ride plans.

Parts of London's past would also participate in the project. Historic locations would be included such as Hyde Park for the triathlon and a new Wembley Stadium due to be completed in 2006 for soccer. There are also a multitude of activities to occur around the festivities of the Games. Various multi-cultural arts and entertainment celebrations have been planned throughout London's many parks and open spaces as part of a simultaneous Olympic Festival to accompany the Games themselves.

Organizers in the Big Apple have opted to begin their strategy by looking to the alphabet. New York's Olympic X Plan situates most of the venues at the intersection of two possible transport routes, one by water and one by rail, which would run through the center of the city. The athletes would be the focus for providing convenience in commuting. The center of the X would be the Olympic Village located across the East River from the UN. There are also a variety of other options that would be available to the participants. For the athletes, there would be expedited Olympic ferries, dedicated Olympic rail lines, and shuttle buses riding in

Olympic Priority road lanes for time efficient transport to their venues and circumventing any adverse traffic situations. The concentration of the athletic sites may or may not ease traffic conditions. All of the competition venues (excluding some for soccer preliminaries) are expected to be within a 32km (20 mile) radius of the Olympic Village. Others professionals for whom the Olympics would be a job also stand to reap certain transport benefits. The dedicated rail and ferry services would also be available to Olympic officials and the media. If terrestrial options run thin, it would be time to go underground. For the rest of those attending or working the Games, organizers say that every venue is at or near a subway stop. In some cases, this may prove to be the best alternative. All except 3 of the venues at which Olympic Finals would take place are inside the limits of the city. One particular section of the Olympic strategy would call for extensive redevelopment in the city. The New York plan is expected to increase the expansion of Manhattan's far west side with the proposed Olympic Stadium, Olympic Square for public gathering and leisure, and an Olympic Boulevard.

PUBLIC OPINION

It always helps to have the public on-board for such a large-scale event. Local support for the Madrid bid cannot be questioned. Organizers have reported that locals have shown great support for the 2012 bid. In two separate surveys, one in Madrid and one throughout the rest of Spain, conducted in mid-November 2003 with 1,000 respondents each, an overwhelming 88.0% of Madrid citizens and 82.6% of Spaniards nationally were personally in favor of having Madrid host the 2012 Games. The fact that everyday citizens can participate in the event provides an added incentive for supporting the project. It was reported that 42.1% of Madrid residents surveyed said they would volunteer in some capacity to help in the project's success. The people also felt a sense of improving national pride via The Games. The main benefit cited by 91% of the citizens surveyed was to improve the prestige and image of Madrid across the globe.

But the naysayers were bound to pop up, and they did. The environmental group Ecologistas en Acción in January of 2004 claimed that Madrid was the most environmentally polluted capital in Europe. They also questioned the proposed site for the canoe/kayaking competition, Araguez located south of the city, citing that forests would have to be cleared along the Tajo River. In May of 2004, the organizing committee issued the Green Letter, a document created specifically to announce that Madrid was dedicated to a cleaner environment for the Games and beyond. A competition was held in local schools for designing the campaign's logo, which was won by a design depicting an athlete showered in flowers and a tagline that read, "Madrid 2012 complies with the environment".

The public seems to be completely supportive of Moscow 2012. The Moscow organizing committee conducted public opinion polls in partnership with ROMIR research and the Gallup organization in Moscow and throughout Russia in the cities of St. Petersburg, Novosibirsk, Nizhniy Novgorod, Voronezh, Rostov-on-Don, and Yekaterinburg regarding hosting of the Olympics and Paralympics in 2012. Participants were questioned in a couple of different ways. The polls in Moscow were conducted via telephone while for the cities other than Moscow, 2 focus groups were conducted in each city with 4 women and 4 men between the ages to 18 to 60. The two polls took place about a month apart. The nationwide poll involving 1546 individuals was carried out in October 2003 while 1000 Moscow residents participated in a separate poll conducted in November 2003. The findings were rather convincing. In the combined results of these polls it was found that, from those people who participated, 90% of Muscovites and 89% of Russians outside Moscow supported the idea of hosting the 2012 Olympic and Paralympic Games in Moscow. The public also showed faith in those responsible for staging the event. It was found from these investigations that 90% of Russians nationwide and 89% of Muscovites felt that both of the 2012 Olympic events would be properly organized. It was difficult to find any type of local, large-scale, organized opposition to the 2012 Games coming to Moscow.

The majority of those polled in France are in favor of bringing the Games to their capital. On behalf of the Paris organizing committee the Taylor Nelson Sofres Institute conducted polling from November 20 to 23, 2003 by involving 600 individuals from Paris, 800 people from the Ile-de-France region, and 1000 persons from other regions throughout France. It was important to check the local as well as national barometer for support. All participants were over the age of 18. The results indicated that there was more local support than national support. This survey found that, of those polled, 75% of Parisians, 73% of the people representing the Ile-de-France region, and 67% of people across France, were in favor of hosting the 2012 Games.

But, as in any city, there are drawbacks that are worth considering. The threat of continually imminent strikes throughout France does pose a threat to the viability of the Games being held in Paris. And most of all, it is difficult to predict the timing of these work stoppages. To make matters worse, trade unions organized a nationwide strike just as IOC inspectors arrived in Paris for the tour of proposed Olympic sites in March 2005.

British organizers were able to report that public support is present throughout the UK. The London organizing committee enlisted the firm ICM who, in December 2002, conducted a nationwide poll of 3200 participants regarding the Games. Most people questioned were ready to accept the Games. Of those individuals polled, 81% said they thought London should go ahead with the bid itself while 82% were in support of the bid. Nationwide backing was slightly higher. Across the country the participants from Northern Ireland showed the highest backing with 87% in support followed by Scotland with 84%. There were no geographic areas for which results indicated any type of majority disapproval for the project. In all of the regions polled the support did not dip below 75%. The private sector was also questioned regarding their thoughts on the Olympics coming local. In January of 2003, the London Chamber of Commerce polled 300 businesses and it was found that 81% were in support of London hosting the 2012 Games.

There is another side to the coin. There are approximately 350 businesses and some 15,000 employees who stand a chance to get displaced in the Marshgate Lane area of east London whose job areas would be threatened with being wiped out to make room for the Games. An environmental concern has been raised here as well. There have been reports of sporadic protesting along the east London waterways from groups fearing a loss of animal habitat and the destruction of over 500 trees along the water for the sake of the Olympics. Bid planners have looked into this issue and did respond. London's organizers have promised to create more park space than there is currently in response to environmental concerns.

New York organizers were able to show a majority support of the Games coming to their city. In a poll conducted in November 2003 involving 406 people in the city, 73% of New Yorkers supported the Olympic bid for their home city while 18% opposed the project. Public authorities have gotten involved at many levels. The New York State government has guaranteed $250 million to help finance the Games. It would seem that work stoppages would not pose a threat to New York's Olympics. The building and trades unions of New York City have ratified a no-strike pledge for a 10-year period for all projects related to the Olympics. New York 2012 has gotten the private sector involved since the early stages of the bid. The organizing committee and the bid itself have received contributions from over 120 corporations. The different nationalities reflected in the city's population have formed an alliance in support of the bid. More than 360 ethnic organizations have organized a coalition called The Nations of New York, focused on creating an organized effort to channel resources from the various communities throughout the city.

It has been well publicized that not everyone has accepted the 2012 plan. The New York bid has faced opposition from those against displacing residents to allow for redevelopment for the Olympic project as well as New Yorkers and metropolitan area residents who wish not to see the traffic delays or other logistical interruptions they may face as a result of the Games. There is an almost tangible divide between the two sides. There is also a fraction of the public that supports bringing the Olympics to New York but opposes the construction of a west side Olympic Stadium.

FINANCIAL TERMS

Whichever of the five cities wins the bid in July 2005 will receive a $600 million contribution from the IOC. This sum would not be part of the revenue generation figures below. The dollar figures that follow are approximate values, where certain fractions of amounts may not be carried through in all cases.

The Spanish organizers have devised a budget mostly containing private sector financing with public authorities also playing a key monetary role. For the Madrid Olympic organizing committee for the Olympic Games (OCOG), most of the finances for the bid would come from private funding (85%) with public administration (15%) handling the rest of the costs. There are two phases a city needs to go through before it even reaches the stage of host city selection by the IOC. The budget for the initial application process known as Phase I was approximately $5.9 million. The next step came when the city was considered a finalist in the bidding process. After Madrid was chosen as one of the last five candidate cities, it entered the final round candidature process known as Phase II where a budget of $12.7 million was due to kick in to finance activities leading up to the July 2005 IOC decision on the 2012 bid.

But there is more. Should Madrid win the bid, according to estimate reports prepared by the organizers, both the cost of hosting the Games as well as the expected revenues from them total $2,000,125,000. According to the strategy, every penny of the budget would be spent on Games-related activities. Therefore, Madrid is set to break even after hosting the Games. Similar to the budget in the earlier bidding phases, private funding would carry the heavier load as far as financing is concerned with public monies supplementing the remaining portion. The Madrid OCOG plans to distribute its own budget in a 20% public to 80% private funding ratio. Local transportation, road, and civic upgrades would be the responsibility of the relevant public and municipal government agencies. The non-OCOG budget, or infrastructure budget, would be financed in full by the relevant public authorities. National authorities would also have a hand in providing financial support. The Spanish Government, at many levels, is heavily involved in the coordination of finances for the Madrid Games project. Some members of the public authorities would even be part of the OCOG. The national, regional, and municipal governments were due to have representation on the organizing committee itself. All three levels would also offer up their current and future athletic facilities free of charge for use by the organizing committee. This could be in the form of competition, non-competition, or training venues. Another key area for which the OCOG would receive government aid is the vast security operation required for the Olympics. The national government has taken on the responsibility for implementing the Games security plan along with agreeing to waive duties for and to facilitate the import and export of any items required by the IOC, international federations, national Olympic committees and their delegates, media, and sponsors/suppliers in relation to the Olympic Games. The national Olympic body would naturally be in coordination with the newly formed OCOG. If chosen to host the Games, it is planned to have the Spanish Olympic Committee merge into the OCOG for the duration of the project.

There are a number of ways organizers plan to create income for the project. Current estimations by the Madrid OCOG for revenue generation to offset the actual cost of planning and hosting the Games have the bulk of income ($363 million) generated by venue ticket sales during or before the Olympics. Three other sources would contribute substantial income to the development of the Games. Local sponsors are slated to bring in $145 million while subsidies ($130 million) and official suppliers ($145 million) are the remaining estimated hefty individual revenue generators. But the earning stream does not stop there. Additional income is expected to come from licensing (close to $100 million); other sources ($170 million) including accommodation, cultural programs, hospitality village sponsors, sponsorship of activities by the European Union, and financial interest income; donations and sales of assets ($28 million); and $27 million from coins, stamps, and lottery revenue. A cumulative view of these sources helps to put things into perspective. Total revenues from all of these sources are expected to approach two billion dollars. This is on track to roughly match the expenditure figure presented earlier.

The timing of when the tickets are expected to sell shows us that not much of that revenue would be available up front for the OCOG to use. Of the $363 million ticket sales revenue figure, $250 million is expected to come from sales during the two weeks of competition, while $54 million is expected from the opening and closing ceremonies, and $18 million is expected from the opening ceremony dress rehearsal, which normally takes place the night before the actual commencement proceedings for the Games.

The early stages of the Moscow bid were the result of financial cooperation between public authorities and private organizations. The Phase I budget for the Moscow bid was $10.5 million, all of which was financed by the Moscow City Government and the private sector. The next stage of bidding was due to be financed entirely using public funds. The estimated Phase II budget to process the necessary resources for the subsequent steps required for Moscow as a final round candidate city was $14.5 million where the Moscow Government was set to contribute $13.05 million and the Federal Government was to chip in $1.45 million.

The OCOG has provided a figure of how much it would cost to hold the Olympics in their city. The full amount of required funds to host the Games in Moscow according to organizers total $1,784,000,000. They hope to have some capital left after their spending for the Games has been completed. In their OCOG reports comparing estimated expenditures with expected revenue generation, after hosting the 2012 Olympics, Moscow stands to gain $6 million in profits. For the Games budget, the government would play a lesser role in terms of financial contribution as compared to the Phase II budget. Private sources would contribute to 70% of the budget while 30% would come from public resources. Local and national authorities would work together to provide the public funding. Of the public funds, the City of Moscow would provide 80% with the Federal Government picking up the remaining 20% of the budget costs. The city has agreed to help in other ways as well. In the case of funds falling short, the Moscow City Government has agreed to pick up the necessary costs. The responsibility of transportation and communications upgrades or modifications has also been claimed by the city. The City Government has taken on the responsibility to finance any related infrastructure development.

Moscow organizers have outlined a variety of revenue sources to help finance the Olympic effort. Here are just a few. The largest income source is expected to be sponsorship (estimated $825 million); followed by ticket revenue (estimated $150 million); Government support

($120 million); other sources ($95 million) such as commemorative stamps, coins, cultural events, donations, lottery and disposing of assets; and finally, licensing sales of approximately $50 million.

Private funding helped to largely finance the early rounds of bidding for the French Capital. In Paris, the Phase I budget was approximately $4.8 million, which subsequently increased to about $22 million once the city entered Phase II. The second phase usually ends up being costlier than the first. Of these funds roughly 25% was picked up by the City of Paris, the Ile-de-France region and French Government. And the budget was expected to increase slightly from there. The organizers estimated that the application and candidature process would take about $27 million to complete.

Organizers have supplied the quantity of funds required to run the Olympics in their city. The Paris OCOG has estimated that it would cost $2,657,035,000 to pull off the Games in Paris and have outlined multiple sources of revenue that would leave Paris with $1.768 million in surplus. The government would play an active role in helping to build and/or refurbish Olympic venues. Public funds would be fully financing 5 permanent venues, financing 50% for 2 permanent venues, and fully financing the renovation of 3 permanent venues. Organizers here are counting on a good fan turnout to bring in a large slice of the revenue pie. The highest individual income generator is estimated to be ticket sales in excess of $612 million. The next biggest money producer is actually a collection of income sources whose total is expected to exceed the ticket sales figure by over $200 million. Sponsorship (of varying types at the local and international level) is expected to bring in a collective amount of about $828 million. The lucrative "exclusive provider" deals are up next. Official suppliers would contribute around $116 million. The income sources keep on coming. Licensing is presumed to generate slightly over $56 million and lotteries and donations are slated to contribute a little more than $75.5 million. Another source of income is the dissemination of the OCOG's material goods. The disposal of assets is estimated to create over $60 million in revenue. There are additional unspecified revenue generators that would also be at work. The OCOG cites "Other" sources would haul in $308 million. Public authorities have agreed to cover costs for a variety of civic services. The government at no cost would provide public services such as transport, security, and medical services.

Any problems with the budget have been insured as well. France's government has guaranteed coverage for any OCOG budgetary shortfalls.

The local and national governments agreed to take on a primary role when it came time to finance London's application. The budget for the London bid was $19 million for the application phase and $29 million for the candidature phase leading up to the July 2005 decision day. The public authorities were equipped to handle any possible extra funds needed for the first two phases. The UK Government and City of London had agreed to contribute up to $34 million while a figure of $14 million was expected to come from the private sector in the from of cash or in-kind services.

British organizers have announced the dollar figure necessary to stage the Olympics in their home city. According to budget estimates prepared by the London OCOG, it would cost $2,462,000,000 to host the Games in England's Capital. A break-even strategy has been put into place for the budget. Revenue sources have been identified that would cover the entire expenditure and there is no shortfall estimated. Sponsorship stands as the big-ticket item for income generation. Approximately $735 million is expected to come from sponsorships while $290 million is estimated from official suppliers. Fans purchasing tickets would contribute greatly to the cause. Ticket sales are expected to generate $496 million and licensing in the form of merchandise and coin programs is estimated to accumulate $92 million. Public funding is expected to be substantial for this project. The National Government is set to contribute $72 million and the disposal of assets is anticipated to bring in $36 million. Revenue generators unspecified by the OCOG would end up contributing also. About $141 million is predicted from other sources.

Any type of finance crisis looks to be averted thanks to insurance provided by the public bodies. The UK Government has established a guarantee to supplement the necessary funds by setting up a $3.8 billion expenditure fund agreed to by the National and City Governments for use on the Olympic project as well as in the event of an OCOG budget shortfall. The government has reached out to the private sector. Private investment is encouraged, but not mandated, to contribute to this fund. The sites of competition also stand to reap rewards from this nest egg. This fund would be used to help finance many of the Games venue refurbishing and construction costs. Local city upgrades would also be one less thing for the organizers to worry about. The appropriate local or national government authorities, at no cost to the London OCOG, would handle infrastructure expenditures.

The early bidding stages for the New York OCOG were bankrolled using private funds. The Phase I budget for New York was $9.2 million while the Phase II budget was slated to be $13.3 million. This $22.5 million figure for the bid was raised totally from the private sector. But organizers have ideas for supplemental monies to provide a bit of assistance. The OCOG expects to raise some additional funds through a paid membership program and sales of licensed merchandise available to the public.

Organizers have put forth the price tag for the 2012 Olympics in New York City. The New York OCOG reports that it would cost $3,084,300,000 to hold the Games in their city and have worked out their expenditures to match this amount with no shortfall expected. So how does one go about netting $3 billion? In addition to the $600 million IOC grant, organizers have provided several sources of income to generate the necessary capital. The sale of sponsorship rights would bring in the most amount of revenue. Sponsorship is expected rake in over $1.22 billion while ticket sales are predicted to produce $852 million in revenue. Further down list there is licensing. An estimated $117 million is estimated to come from licensing rights. Finally, there are a group of sources that would help fill out the income grid. The OCOG anticipates receiving $75 million in donations, $14.1 million from the disposal of assets, $75 million in Federal Government subsidies, and $228 million from other, as yet unspecified, sources.

Financial guarantees are in place to ensure that a lack of money would not hamper Olympic organizing efforts. The OCOG has obtained a $250 million joint guarantee from the New York State and New York City governments. An additional store of cash also stands at the ready. A general contingency fund of $200 million has been established for the Olympic project.

VENUES OF COMPETITION

In Madrid, approximately 70% of the required competition venues already exist. Travel times between the Olympic Village and any city venue would not exceed 26 minutes. Spectators would have access to 82% of the competition venues via subway or suburban rail. The distance between any competition venue (excluding rowing, canoe/kayak, and sailing) and the Olympic Village would not exceed 20 km. Most of the venues, regardless of if they were temporary or permanent, would require some type of temporary refurbishing during early 2012 in the majority of cases.

There are 9 existing venues in the East Sector, which are capable of accommodating 11 sports. The 75,000-seat Madrid Stadium, constructed in 1994 at a cost of almost $160 million of public funding, would host athletics competitions and is undergoing a two-year renovation, which is set to be complete in 2006. Seven pavilions located on the IFEMA trade fair grounds, ranging in seating capacity from 2,000 to 8,000 would host fencing, weightlifting, boxing, badminton, taekwondo, table tennis, wrestling, and judo. Some refurbishing would be required here. These pavilions are scheduled to undergo minor upgrades in 2011 using both public and private funding. A moderate sized stadium for baseball would also be located in this sector. The 8,000-capacity Rivas Vaciamadrid Baseball Center, opened in 1999 and would be renovated from 2008 to 2011 at a public cost of $70 million, would hold the baseball and softball competitions.

Along the Central Axis, there are 4 currently standing venues that can host 3 competitions. Two of the structures are familiar to most locals and have been so for quite some time. The historic 90,000 capacity Santiago Bernabéau Stadium originally built for club team Real Madrid in 1947 and renovated in 2001 would be the site for the soccer preliminaries and final while, at half the capacity of Bernabéau, Vicente Calderon Stadium, which was originally built in 1966 as the home of Real's cross-town rivals Atletico Madrid, would serve as host for the soccer preliminaries. But they have logged their share of matches. Both of these stadiums would need upgrades in 2011 of roughly $2.3 million each, which would be privately financed. The Felipe II Sports Hall, a 14,500-seat arena that began construction in 2001 and opened in 2004 costing the Spanish public in excess of $114 million, would be the venue for team handball. Another baseball venue has actually been around for quite some time. La Elipa is a 5,000-seat baseball stadium constructed in 1958 and would be refurbished in 2011. Then there is that venue which has virtually no boundaries. The Madrid City Circuit for road cycling would be constructed in 2012 at a relatively low cost of $589,050 to be derived from public funds.

The West Sector is where a group of publicly funded venues stand today ready to a variety of competitions. The hoops facility is fairly recent in existence. The Rockódromo Arena took two years and over $86 million to build before opening in 2004 as a 12,000-seat basketball arena. The horses of Madrid 2012 would be treading on historic ground. Opened in 1936, the 15,200-capacity Zarzuela Racetrack, the planned equestrian venue, is currently undergoing a $29 million two-year facelift to be completed in 2006. The 2,000-seat Casa de Campo Triathlon Venue and Cycling Circuit were introduced in 1977 and are scheduled to receive an $8 million upgrade between 2010 and 2012. A 73-year old facility is set to welcome a series of outdoor events. The venue for hockey, archery, and the modern pentathlon, the 12,000 capacity Club de Campo Villa de Madrid, opened in 1932 and is scheduled for a two year $7 million renovation project beginning in 2010.

There would be additional facilities participating domestically. Five other "sub-venues" are already in place throughout the rest of Spain. Most of these would serve as venues for soccer. Four of these sub-venues: José Rico Perez Stadium in Alicante, Montjuic Olympic Stadium (site of Barcelona 1992), Arcangel Municipal Stadium in Córdoba, and La Rosaleda Stadium in Málaga are private structures slated to hold preliminary rounds of the Olympic soccer tournament. How about a venue whose age cannot be estimated without the help of a geologist? Probably the oldest venue for the Madrid Games would be the Bay of Palma de Mallorca, planned to be host of the sailing competition and would require over $10 million of public monies for the construction of a 2,000 spectator capacity structure.

Taxpayer money would be used for the building of certain venues. There are publicly funded venues currently in the early development stages, two of which are already under construction. Aquatics and volleyball are being addressed on the East side of town. Located in the East Sector are the Olympic Aquatic Center for swimming, diving, and water polo holding a combined 23,000 plus spectators at a cost of over $147 million whose four-year construction project began in 2003, and the Coslada Volleyball Complex, a 12,000-seat arena expensed at over $56 million for which a two year construction plan gets underway in 2008. Three-year construction began in 2003 for the Manzanares Park Tennis Center in the Central Axis consisting of a central stadium holding 12,000 plus and two side courts holding 5,000 and 3,000 fans. The price tag for this nudges slightly over $140 million. The city would also see the construction of the Aranjuez Flatwater Canal for rowing and canoe/kayak (flatwater), which would accommodate 10,000 spectators and would cost over $70 million for which construction is set to run from 2005 to 2007.

Not all venues are without contingency. There are five additional venues which would be constructed should Madrid receive the bid. Once again, it's the taxpayers to the rescue. All of these venues would be publicly funded, would be located in the East Sector, and require two years each to construct. The Olympic Pavilion, a 20,000 seat gymnastics (artistic and rhythmic) arena would begin construction in 2006 and cost just under $50 million. The Olympic Ring Velodrome for track cycling is a $23 million, 5,000-seat temporary complex planned for construction in 2008. The 12,000 seat Coslada Volleyball Complex would be augmented in 2006 to include a temporary beach volleyball court, named Juan Carlos I Park, at a cost of $12 million. The Olympic Shooting Range – Paracuellos would be a $23 million, 5,000-seat center that could begin building in 2005. A whitewater canal located in the La Gavia Park, seating 8,000 spectators for canoe/kayak (slalom) would also begin construction in 2005 and cost over $11 million.

The center of Moscow's competition venue plan is actually made up of the non-competition venues of the Olympic Village, MPC, IBC, and the Media Village. Within a 5 km radius of this central point, there are five compounds of sport. The CSKA Football Stadium, the historic home to the local soccer club of the same name, is a 50,000-seat facility slated for a two-year construction project from 2005 to 2007. The CSKA Sports Complex is a 5,000-capacity arena for taekwondo, judo and fencing which was originally built in 1980 and is scheduled for a two-year renovation starting in 2009. The Dynamo Sports Complex consists of the 45,000-seat Dynamo Stadium for soccer; originally constructed in 1928 for the Dynamo Moscow soccer club, renovated in 1979, and is scheduled for two years of further upgrades starting in 2009. This complex also houses a 5,000 capacity handball arena currently undergoing two years of construction set to be completed in 2006. To the south of the center point, is the awe inspiring Luzhniki Sports Complex, all of its facilities originally built in 1957, which is comprised of an 80,000 capacity stadium that has experienced renovations in 1979 and 2000, and has scheduled upgrades from 2009 to 2011; an 8,500 capacity multi-purpose hall that was refurbished in 1979 and is set to be renovated again for two years beginning in 2008; a 12,500 seat sports palace also renovated in 1979 and undergoing repairs from 2005 to 2012; and an 18,500 seat spectator capacity swimming pool currently undergoing three years of renovations until 2007. There is also a 15,000-seat hockey center which would undergo a private $21.9 million renovation in 2011. Luzhniki would be the site of the Olympic Park as well as the Opening and Closing Ceremonies. Sporting competitions to take place at Luzhniki include soccer, athletics, badminton, boxing, field hockey, and wrestling. Directly west of the Village/Media complex is the Krylatskoye Sports Complex. This facility consists of an indoor cycling track accommodating 6,000 spectators originally built in 1980 and is set to be refurbished for one year in 2009; an outdoor cycling track constructed in 1980 and scheduled to be renovated from 2009 to 2011; a rowing channel able to seat 2,000 which was introduced in 1980 and would undergo a two-year renovation starting in 2009; and two temporary venues seating 5,000 each for rowing/ triathlon and shooting to be constructed between 2005 and 2011. There is also the planned construction in 2011 of a temporary 8,000 capacity baseball stadium at a price of $19 million covered by the government. Krylatskoye would host the sports of rowing, baseball, both flatwater and slalom canoe/kayak, cycling, triathlon, weightlifting, and table tennis. There is also the planned construction of the Novko Sports Palace for gymnastics between 2004 and 2006 at a private cost of $79 million.

Between 5 and 10 km from the Village/Complex there are five competition facilities. Facing east from the center point, constructed in 1980, and scheduled for upgrades from 2008 to 2011, is the Olympiskiy Sports Complex with its 18,500-seat multi-sports indoor arena and 6,000 capacity indoor swimming pool arena. In addition to the aquatic events of diving, synchronized swimming and water polo, this complex is slated to host basketball and volleyball. About 8 km south of the Olympic Village is the Spartak Football Stadium, home of the well-known Spartak

Moscow soccer club team, holding 50,000 spectators with two-year construction of the facility beginning in 2005. To the northwest of the Village/Media nucleus is the brand new Tushino Sports Complex with new facilities that would be erected between 2008 and 2012. This complex would have a 10,000-seat baseball stadium, as well as two planned temporary venues in the form of an 8,500-viewer softball stadium and a beach volleyball facility accommodating 5,000 people. In addition there is planned construction for the $122 million privately financed Tushino Football Stadium with ground breaking set for late 2005. In the compound would also be a temporary 5,000-spectator archery field costing $2.8 million in public funds to be constructed in 2011 and a temporary 5,000 capacity shooting range planned to be built in 2011 at a cost of $3.10 million of government funding. Sports to be competed at Tushino include soccer, softball, beach volleyball, archery, shooting, and baseball. Northeast of Tushino, the all-new 12,000-spectator J.A. Samaranch Tennis Center is scheduled to begin its two-year construction in 2005 at a private cost of $49 million.

There are three venues located between 10 and 20 km from the Village/Media hub. East of the midpoint is the 30,000-seat Lokomotiv Football Stadium, opened in 2000 for the FC Lokomotiv soccer club and would have minor touch ups in 2011. Southeast of the core is the Bitza Horseracing Complex (for equestrian and modern pentathlon), holding 1200 fans, which was built in 1980 and would require three years of refurbishing starting in 2005 at a private cost of $49 million. Due west of Bitza is the proposed $32 million government financed mountain biking venue of Novoperedelkino which would be a natural terrain venue constructed in 2010.

The only remaining venue is the Klyazma Sailing Center located a little over 20 km north of the Olympic Village. This was introduced in 1995 and is under a seven-year $150 million (50% government funds and 50% private funds) renovation period that began in 2004.

The venue organization for Paris consists of 9 venues in the Northern Cluster, 8 venues in the Western Cluster, 9 venues scattered throughout the Ile-de-France region, and 5 venues throughout the rest of France. Most of the venues, regardless of if they were temporary or permanent, would require some type of temporary refurbishing (during early 2012 in the majority of cases) which would be financed by the OCOG budget.

The Northern Cluster would contain 3 permanent venues and 6 temporary venues. The 71,000-seat Stade de France, which hosted the 1998 World Cup Finals, would be used as the Olympic Stadium in 2012 hosting athletics, soccer, as well as the opening and closing ceremonies. This is the only existing venue in this cluster and would have a $3.6 million renovation financed by the OCOG in 2012 in preparation for the Games. The brand new Aquatic Center, holding 20,000 spectators for swimming and synchronized swimming and 5,000 viewers each for diving and water polo, would cost $51.6 million in public funds. This would be a permanent venue for all four aquatic sports whose two-year construction would begin in 2009. The permanent venue of the SuperDome, to be used for artistic and rhythmic gymnastics as well as trampoline, would be a new construction at a price of $385.6 million (74% public funding and 26% private funding) completing three years of building in 2011 and would be capable of holding 22,000 audience members. There would be 6 temporary venues fully financed by the OCOG called Pavilion 1 through 6, that would accommodate the sports of basketball, boxing, weightlifting, table tennis, wrestling, taekwondo, and handball, which would range in seating capacity from 5,000 to 17,000 and be constructed from 2010 to 2012.

There would be 5 permanent venues and 3 temporary venues in the Western Cluster. Four of these venues already exist. The historic Roland Garros Tennis Stadium, originally built in 1928, famous for hosting the annual French Open with its main court holding 14,140 fans and its multiple side courts holding 15,200 total fans, would require a three-month, $800,000 temporary remodeling in 2012. The longtime home of the pro soccer club Paris St. Germain is the 48,500 capacity Parc des Prince, originally constructed in 1972, which would require a temporary refurbishing costing $900,000 taking place over a four-month period in 2012. The Jean-Bouin Stadium with a main field holding 15,000 spectators and a side field holding 5,000 for field hockey was opened in 1916 and would need a one year fixing starting in 2008 at a cost of $28.6 million in public money. A permanent 15,000-seat Dome Arena for judo and badminton costing 104.4 million dollars in combined public and private funds would be constructed from 2009 to 2011. The Longchamp Bagatelle, holding 30,000 (with a total grounds capacity of 50,000) for equestrian and modern pentathlon would be a temporary venue built for two years starting in 2010 at a cost of $33 million in OCOG money. The other modern pentathlon venue would be the Croix Catelan, an already existing (3,000-capacity each for shooting, fencing and swimming) venue built first in 1886, would require a one year, $5.5 million private renovation starting in 2008. The 5,000-spectator Auteuil Racecourse would be a temporary $8.9 million OCOG funded venue for archery and would be constructed over four months in early 2012. A new Pavilion 7 for fencing would be a temporary 10,000-seat venue constructed between 2011 and 2012 using $24.4 million in OCOG finances.

The non-cluster venues would include 5 permanent venues and 4 temporary venues situated at other locations throughout Paris. Two of the venues currently exist. The Eiffel Tower would undergo a temporary $8.8 million OCOG funded renovation in 2012 to accommodate the triathlon, marathon, and the cycling time trial as well as 5,000 spectators. The Champ-de-Mars for beach volleyball would be a temporary venue costing $9.9 million in OCOG money and would be capable of holding 10,000 fans. Volleyball would be played in the 12,500-seat Paris Bercy Dome, originally constructed in 1984, which would be renovated for 3 years ending in 2011 at a price tag of $3 million in public funds. The Vaires-sur-Marne Regatta Center, opened in 1990, would be the venue for rowing and canoe/kayak. This facility, to be completed in 2006 requiring $12 million in additions/renovations via public funding, would hold 21,800 for flatwater competitions and 10,000 for the slalom events. Track cycling and mountain biking would take place at the new St. Quentin-en-Yvelines Velodrome and Park, which would be two permanent venues at a public cost of around $48 million and would be ready by 2011. The velodrome would hold 6,000 while the park would hold 5,000. The Palace of Versailles would be the starting point for road cycling and would undergo a temporary $8 million OCOG funded renovation to hold 5,000 spectators. A brand new permanent venue for shooting, the 3,000-seat Versailles Shooting Center, would be built at a public cost of $14.3 million from 2009 to 2011. The Colombes Sports Center, consisting of 10,000- and 5,000-capacity fields for baseball and an 8,000 capacity field for softball, would be a temporary venue at an OCOG cost of $25.9 million.

Permanent venues located in other provinces throughout France include 4 existing soccer stadiums (Marseille, Lyon, Nantes, and Lens) ranging in capacity from 38,000 to 60,000 that would require minimal (under $1million) OCOG funded temporary modifications in 2012 as well as the Les Minimes Port at La Rochelle, the 4,000-spectator sailing venue originally opened in 1971 requiring $6.1 million in OCOG funded renovations to be completed in 2012.

For the London project, there are 17 existing venues that would be utilized during the Games. There would also be 8 new permanent competition venues constructed and 7 temporary venues would be made if London were awarded the Olympics in 2012. Most of the venues, regardless of if they were temporary or permanent, would require some type of temporary refurbishing (during early 2012 in the majority of cases) which would be financed by the OCOG budget.

There are 15 existing venues for which no permanent works are required. The modifications on these venues in the months leading up to the Games would be financed by the OCOG, would range from $0.2 million to $38 million, and would total $105 million. The soccer venues falling under this category include: a new 90,000-seat Wembley Stadium currently under construction in London due to be completed in 2006; Hampden Park in Glasgow seating 52,000 which was built in 1903 and renovated in 1994; the 75,000-capacity Old Trafford in Manchester (built in 1910 and refurbished in 1995); Millennium Stadium in Cardiff holding 74,600, constructed in 1999; the 52,000-seat St. James' Park in Newcastle, which was opened in 1892 and renovated in 1992; as well as the 42,000-spectator capacity

Villa Park in Birmingham. The Lord's Cricket Ground, a 6,500-capacity structure built in 1815 and renovated in 1999, would be the venue for archery. The Dome, opened in 1999, would hold the artistic gymnastics events and the basketball final. The ExCel, its two halls holding 6,000 and 10,000 spectators each, opened in 2000, is located adjacent to the London City Airport and would host boxing, judo, table tennis, taekwondo, wrestling, and weightlifting. Mountain Biking would take place at the Weald Country Park in East London with a seating capacity of 3,000. The 23,000-capacity Greenwich Park in East London would be the site for equestrian and modern pentathlon. The world famous 30,000-total capacity Wimbledon would be the site for the tennis competition. Hyde Park would be able to accommodate 3,000 folks for the triathlon. Horse Guards Parade, in the Whitehall section of London, would be the 17,000-total capacity beach volleyball venue. Regent's Park in the West End of London would be the centerpiece of the road cycling race and would accommodate 3,000 seated fans.

There are 2 existing venues where $15 million in permanent works financed from the $3.8 billion government-funding package would be necessary. Weymouth and Portland on England's South Coast for sailing, opened in

1970, would require $6 million and one year to be upgraded to a 240-seat facility by 2011. The venue for rowing/canoe/ kayak (flatwater) would be the 20,000-seat Eton Dorney, 25 miles west of London, which was built in 2000 and would be scheduled for a one-year renovation ending in 2006 at a cost of $9 million.

For the 8 new permanent competition venues to be built in the event of a winning bid, the price tag would be $922 million coming from the aforementioned government-funding package. The planned 20,000-seat, $117 million Aquatics Center to be situated in the Olympic Park would be built from 2005 to 2008 for hosting the aquatics competitions. The Olympic Stadium for athletics and the opening/closing ceremonies would be an 80,000-seat facility in the heart of the Olympic Park and whose construction would last three years at a cost of $450 million. For handball, the 10,000-seat Olympic Park Arena 3 would be constructed for two years ending in 2011 costing $42 million. The Broxbourne Canoe Stadium in Hertfordshire for canoe/kayak (slalom) would be a 12,000-spectator $15 million facility slated to start a two-year construction project in 2006. A $46 million, one year building project commencing in 2007 would be required for the 6,000-seat Olympic Park Velodrome for track cycling. The 6,000-spectator Olympic Park BMX Circuit would be a one-year project ending in 2008 with a price tag of $13 million. Also in the Park would be the Olympic Park Hockey Center, with two fields of 15,000- and 5,000-capacity, that would be built over one year ending in 2011 at a cost of $23 million. Regent's Park would be utilized for softball where a $1 million field seating 8,000 would be created in 2011.

A total of 7 temporary venues would be constructed between 2010 and 2012 with joint funding from the OCOG ($81 million) and the government-funding package ($164 million). Regents Park would host baseball on 15,000- and 5,000-capacity fields costing $21 million. Olympic Park Arenas 1 (Volleyball, 12,000 seats), 2 (Basketball, 12,000 seats), and 4 (Fencing, 4,000 seats) would cost $52 million, $48 million, and $34 million, respectively. The UEL Docklands to be used for water polo would cost $32 million to be converted to accommodate 5,000 spectators. For badminton and rhythmic gymnastics there would be the Greenwich Arena holding 6,000 and costing $26 million. The Royal Artillery Barracks at Woolwich is the venue for shooting where 7,500 spectators could be seated. The modifications on the Barracks for Games purposes would total $32 million.

New York's 2012 Olympic plan has the majority of venues (17 sports) situated within a 10 km radius of the Olympic Village which would be located in Queens across the East River from the United Nations. All of the venues (excluding certain soccer preliminary sites) would be within 32km of the Village. Most of the venues would run along two routes intersecting at the Village forming an "X" across New York City. There are three main clusters of venues that are part of the "X": the Olympic Square Cluster on the west side of Manhattan to host 8 sports, the Olympic Park Cluster east of the Olympic Village in Queens to host 6 events, and the Olympic Riverfront Cluster covering the northern tip of Manhattan and the south Bronx to host 4 sports. Venues would be positioned in all 5 of New York City's boroughs: Brooklyn, The Bronx, Manhattan, Queens, and Staten Island; as well as Long Island in New York state, and East Rutherford in the state of New Jersey. Most of the venues, regardless of if they were temporary or permanent, would require some type of temporary refurbishing (during early 2012 in the majority of cases) which would be financed by the OCOG budget.

Brooklyn would be home to 3 venues. The planned Brooklyn Arena, a 16,000-seat arena for rhythmic, artistic, and trampoline gymnastics, would be constructed for three years starting in 2005 at a cost of $650 million in private funding. At Williamsburg Waterfront Park would be the Olympic Aquatic Center, a temporary venue costing $95.7 million ($80 million public and $15.7 million OCOG funding). The venue, slated for a two-year construction ending in 2011, would hold 16,500 spectators for swimming, synchronized swimming, and the water polo finals; 10,000 for diving; and 5,000 for the water polo preliminaries. Also at Williamsburg would be the temporary Olympic Beach Volleyball Arena, a 14,500-capacity structure to be built in 2012 using $4 million in public financing.

There would be 4 venues situated in the Bronx. The historic Yankee Stadium, home to the internationally renowned Yankees baseball team, would require no permanent modifications and would hold 57,500 fans for the baseball competition. Pelham Bay Park would be home to The Olympic Shooting Center, an existing facility that would require a $34.1 million OCOG-financed makeover from 2009 to 2011 to house 9,700 patrons. Also at Pelham Park would be the Olympic Modern Pentathlon Center, a temporary 8,800-seat venue, which would be financed by the OCOG at $11.4 million and would be erected in 2012. Track cycling and badminton would be held at the Bronx Olympic Velodrome and Arena, a $68.4 million permanent facility to be bankrolled entirely by the OCOG and seating 5,600 for cycling and 8,200 for badminton that would begin two year construction in 2007.

Manhattan would house 6 competition venues. The 369th Regiment Arena is an existing facility for boxing that would require a $12 million OCOG financed overhaul between 2009 and 2011 allowing 10,200 spectators to be seated. The 18,000-seat Olympic Hockey Center would incorporate Columbia University's Baker Field for which the OCOG would finance $10.1 million in renovations. Central Park would be temporarily utilized as a venue for the triathlon whose seated spectator capacity would be 5,000 but whose standing viewer capacity would be far greater than that. The Javitz Convention Center is an existing structure that would host 6 Olympic sports. For weightlifting (5,000 seating capacity), judo (8,400 seating capacity), wrestling (8,400 seating capacity), table tennis (6,500 seating capacity), and taekwondo (5,700 seating capacity), the center's existing facilities would undergo minor, temporary modifications. Permanent refurbishing of the Javitz courtesy of $505 million in government funds would be required to host the fencing competition with construction scheduled for five years ending in 2010. Historic Madison Square Garden, holding 18,600 fans, would host the basketball tournament and would not require any permanent works. The 78,000-seat Olympic Stadium would be a brand new $1.4 billion privately and publicly funded facility to be constructed from 2005 to 2008 and would host athletic events, the soccer final, as well as both the Opening and Closing Ceremonies.

The borough of Queens would contain 6 Olympic venues. The Gateway Park Olympic Marina would be a new $17.9 million OCOG-funded sailing venue capable of accommodating from 3,500 to thousands of spectators and whose one-year construction project would begin in 2010. Corona Park would be home to the temporary 5,000-capacity Olympic Archery Field at Flushing Meadows. The planned Olympic Water Polo Center at Flushing Meadows Corona Park would be a permanent 5,000-seat arena costing the government $60 million and would be used during the Games for the water polo preliminaries. Also at Corona Park, there would be the newly constructed permanent Olympic Regatta Center at Flushing Meadows seating 25,000 for rowing and flatwater canoe/kayak, with an estimated price tag of $67.1million paid for by the OCOG to be built for three years commencing in 2006. Rounding out the Corona Park venues is the Olympic Whitewater Center at Flushing Meadows, to be a new $18.5 million OCOG-funded 15,000-seat facility for slalom canoe/kayak to be constructed for two years staring in 2007. The National Tennis Center, already hosting the annual US Open grand slam event, would provide a 23,000-seat facility with side courts and would require no permanent upgrades.

Staten Island would hold 4 venues. The Greenbelt Olympic Equestrian Center would be a permanent $28.2 million OCOG-financed facility holding 32,000 patrons to be built from 2009 to 2011. The Staten Island Olympic Cycling Center would be a new permanent $41 million government-funded facility and would hold 15,000 for mountain biking and 7,500 for BMX with four years of construction planned to begin in 2005. The Richmond County Olympic Softball Stadium is an existing venue with no required permanent works and a viewer capacity of 11,100 people. Fort Wadsworth would be the temporary venue for road cycling able to hold from 1,700 to thousands of spectators along the course.

Outside of New York City, Long Island and New Jersey would also participate in the Games. The Nassau Coliseum, longtime home to the Islanders professional ice hockey team, would serve as the 16,200-seat Olympic Handball Arena and would not require any permanent construction. Across the Hudson River in New Jersey, the existing 77,600-seat Giants Stadium and 19,400-seat Arena at the Meadowlands

Sports Complex would host the Olympic soccer and volleyball (indoor and beach) tournaments, respectively. The soccer preliminaries would also be hosted at existing stadiums in Philadelphia, Landover (near Washington D.C.), and Foxborough (near Boston).

VENUES OF NON-COMPETITION

Housing for the athletes is usually designed for optimal convenience and the shortest possible commuting times. The Olympic Village in Madrid is planned for construction approximately 600m away from the heart of the Olympics in the Spanish Capital, the Olympic Ring. The magnitude of foreign participants was also taken into consideration. The Village is situated 5 minutes away from the Barajas Airport and 12 minutes from central Madrid. Most of the incoming athletes would not know their way around the city. This is why various modes of public transport would be located within walking distance of the housing. The space to build the facility has already been secured with local authorities. The 85-hectare Village sprawl is one part of 250 hectares of public land set to be developed by the Madrid City Council. The style of housing has also been determined. The complex would be comprised of houses and apartments not exceeding five stories in height, with a minimum of two beds, air conditioning in all rooms, as well as accessibility for use by Paralympic athletes and officials. But the area is not limited to just living space. On-site would be a medical clinic, training facilities, and recreation areas. Financial backing has been put into place that would ensure advantages for local residents beyond the Olympics. The Village would be bankrolled using public and private funds with residential buildings to be converted into public housing and private property sales after the Games. The education sector would also be rewarded from the project. A portion of the Village would subsequently become part of a university campus. But not all of the events would take place in Madrid. For those sports requiring sub-venues away from the city such as soccer and sailing, hotel exclusivity would be obtained for the participating athletes and officials. Non-athletes who are part of a national contingent would have limited living space next to the athletes' accommodation. Additional officials would be provided with annex housing adjacent to the Olympic Village with similar amenities.

Planning for the immense media coverage of the Games has also been laid out. The International Media Center, comprised of the IBC and MPC, would be part of an extension to the IFEMA fair grounds in the East Sector. The broadcast and press professionals would have two distinct facilities. These two areas would be kept separate to ensure efficiency. However, their proximity next to each other may allow for the use of common infrastructure services such as catering, transport, media representative hospitality areas, and sharing of information and results. The central location relative to the venues of competition throughout the city was a major advantage in selecting this site for the media centers. The multiple sporting events that are to be held right in the IFEMA complex would minimize and in some cases, eliminate, the commute from the IBC or MPC to the field of play for the accredited journalists. Accommodation for the journalists would be available in close proximity. The trade fair grounds offer a large number of hotels in the immediate surroundings that would be set-aside for members of the media covering the Games. The centers would have a lasting effect on the immediate infrastructure. After the Olympics, these facilities would remain active participants in future conventions and conferences taking place in Madrid. The current structure would have to be augmented in the event Madrid wins the Games and requires the construction of this media center. Funding for this upgrade has been taken care of for the organizers. The fair grounds extension that would serve as the heart of the Olympic coverage would be financed by IFEMA, which owns and operates the grounds. The Madrid City Council, Madrid Chamber of Commerce, Madrid Regional Government, and the banking group of Caja Madrid form the IFEMA.

In Moscow, the athletes and media would be located close to one another. In the Russian Capital, the Olympic Village is planned to be located in a prestigious area of northwest Moscow within walking distance to the IBC and MPC. The Village would also provide for officials to be included with the athletes. The 80-hectare plot would provide living space for 20,000 athletes, coaches and officials. Funding and land space has already been cleared with the local government. The Village would be financed privately and would occupy previously unused land provided by the City Government. Urban-style housing would be incorporated into the design. The core of the Village would be a collection of 15 apartment buildings ranging from 3 to 22 stories, amidst scenic green lawn space. The Village would also be designed in a manner that is accessible for the Paralympic athletes and officials. Commuting times were taken into consideration when choosing the location. From the Village, most competition and non-competition venues would be within 15-20 minutes by bus. The local economy would be served in the future.

Post 2012, these residences would be sold off as private real estate. Housing for events outside the city is being looked at currently. Short-term accommodations for the sailing venue are in the planning stages.

The location of the broadcast hub would not be far at all. Within walking distance of the Olympic and Media Village would be the IBC. Studio space as well as offices would be provided in the facility. This new construction is planned to be a five story, 70,000 square meter structure located upon 20 hectares of land. Additional technologic services would be available on-site. The facility would have its own ancillary infrastructure as well as uninterrupted power supply, communication connections, security, and parking. The IBC would be privately funded and subsequently could be used by other private entities for media or office purposes.

The press would not be too far away. Adjacent to the IBC would be the MPC with its 40,000 square meters of floor space accommodating around 1,200 press personnel. Complete supplementary services would be incorporated into the building. The brand new facility is expected to have its own photo lab, publishing house, and a press conference room seating 1,000. The MPC would also be privately financed.

Athletes for the Games in France would be able to choose which way they want to go. The Olympic Village in Paris would be located at a central point forming the vertex between the North and West Clusters. Taking either direction would bring them to a collection of sporting venues. It would be situated in the Batignolles district of the 17th arrondisement of Paris, 6 km from each of the main clusters. The permission to potentially use this area of land for the facility has been obtained. The Village, spread out over 34.5 hectares and including ample park space, would house 17,000 athletes and officials. Three public agencies currently control the land in question. The site for the Village is owned by a combination of the City of Paris, the French Government, and the Public Railways Corporation. Apartment-style living would adorn the plot. The Village would also be designed in a manner that is accessible for the Paralympic athletes and officials. Most of the accommodations would be new 8 story buildings, which would continue as residential space following the Games. A joint public/private effort would be put forth to finance the construction. The project would cost over $2 billion of which $860 million would be used for new housing construction with 60% private funding and 40% public monies.

A satellite accommodation center is in the works for participants requiring housing away from Paris. An ancillary Village similar to the main facility would be constructed at La Rochelle for the sailing competition. For the rest of the sites, existing accommodations would be held especially for the Olympic Family. Hotels meeting the standards of the Village would be made exclusively available at the soccer sites throughout France.

The media complex would be a pair of buildings serving both the broadcast and press needs. The IBC and MPC would be situated in two adjacent facilities on a 12-hectare site in the Northern Cluster as permanent buildings. Accommodation for the media has also been planned carefully. There would be a 300-room hotel next door exclusively available to the members of the media. The athletic hub of the Games would be in close proximity. The media complex would be located 300 meters away from the Olympic Stadium and have a dedicated pedestrian route leading there from the media center. The broadcast compound would actually be a collection of facilities acting as one. The IBC would be a 60,000 square meter facility consisting of 7 buildings connected by covered corridors. Press operations would be conducted out of a single edifice. The MPC would be a 3 story office building covering

30,000 square meters. Ancillary services would be provided under a group of pavilions. There would be shared services buildings scattered around these structures for things such as dining, banking, shopping etc. In the future this area would be transitioned into the local business community. After the Olympics these facilities would become office buildings. Funding for the two media centers is due to come from different sources. The IBC is due to be funded by the OCOG while the MPC would be bankrolled by a combination of public and private funds.

The Olympic Park in London would serve as the centerpiece of Olympic activity in 2012. In East London, at the heart of the Olympic Park, would be the Olympic Village. Downtime activities such as shopping and entertainment would be available in close proximity. The location leaves visitors 7 minutes from central London and directly next to Stratford City, an area of new retail and commercial development. London's plan offers a unique augmentation capability in terms of quantity of rooms that could be made available for housing. The facility would have 17,320 beds for athletes and officials with the flexibility to add more if necessary. The athletes' places of work would be at a convenient distance. According to the OCOG, 80% of the Olympic and 95% of the Paralympic athletes would be 20 minutes or less from their competition venues. Finances have been secured for the building of this facility, which would be made accessible for the Paralympic athletes and officials as well. The Village is a $1.04 billion project that would be funded by a public and private sector consortium with a funding guarantee from the Mayor of London. Organizers would have to pay rental fees for the duration of their use. The cost to the OCOG for renting this facility is capped at $40 million. The relevant authorities have approved the land and area for this project. The plot would cover 30 hectares and would include apartment-style living ranging from 2 people per room to 9 people per room. The post-Olympic use would benefit the local community. The site, which is currently owned by the public sector, would become affordable housing in the future. Beyond the city, organizers have planned alternate but similar housing solutions as the ones available in London. Equivalent or better housing accommodations would be made available for those athletes competing at venues outside of London.

The media center would also be close by. The new IBC and MPC would be linked facilities located inside the Olympic Park. The buildings would occupy no more than 2 floors. The single story IBC would cover 65,000 square meters while the 2 story MPC would occupy 45,000 square meters. Organizers are looking to provide broadcasters with unique vistas as they beam the Games to the world. Rooftop studios would provide the first-ever live backdrop setting with a direct view of the Olympic Stadium and Olympic Park for exclusive coverage for rights holders. Organizers would have a choice of where to hold the press conferences. The facility would have 4 press briefing rooms, one of 200 seats and three others of 50 seats each. Ancillary facilities would also be included in the package. The complex would have photo services, food courts, and bars on premises. Housing exclusivity would provide assistance to the throngs of media members due to cover the Games. In addition to the exclusive Bloomsbury hotels for print journalists and photographers in central London, designated media hotels would be available near the Olympic Park. Journalists would also receive some very useful perks. All public transport would be free for media members and a full service Olympic transport service would be available from the IBC/MPC. Funding for this project has been approved and is ready to take action should London win the bid. The facility would cost approximately $215 million and would be financed from the $3.8 billion government-funding package.

Athlete housing in New York City would offer riverfront views and a picturesque photo opportunity of the famous city skyline. Located in Queens across from the UN would be the Olympic Village, positioned along the East River's waterfront 3km from Times Square. Officials have carefully planned out convenience of commuting. An OCOG report states that athletes would be no more than 21 minutes from their competition venues by shuttle buses using dedicated Olympic lanes and would also be able to use the ferry system. Most of the land to be used for this project has been secured. The Queens West Development Corporation, a government agency, controls development of this 25 hectare area while a smaller section to the east of the site would be purchased as part of the project. A variety of styles would be incorporated into the housing facilities. Approximately 4,400 low- and high-rise apartments of 28 square meters of living space each would be constructed. An additional 200 apartments would be available adjacent to the Village for extra officials. The Village would be designed in a manner that is accessible for the Paralympic athletes and officials. The facility would also hold a purpose after serving the Olympics. After the Games, these apartments would be leased or sold as private housing. The government would not have to contribute directly to the building of these apartments. In total, the Village is an approximately $1.6 billion privately funded, permanent project whose construction is planned to take place between 2007 and 2012. The OCOG would be outlaying $60.6 million in temporary works for the Olympic Village.

The media centers would be situated in another borough. The IBC and MPC would be located in Manhattan adjacent to the Olympic Stadium in the largest cluster of events at the Games. The plans for the broadcast facility are quite extensive. The IBC would be a privately funded $360 million, 93,000 square meter facility inside the new 45-story Olympic Tower whose building is planned from 2009 to 2011. Space would not be a problem here. The IBC would take up the first 4 floors with the bottom 2 used for logistics and information booths while the third and fourth floors would serve as the first line of studios for the larger broadcast rights holders. From there, one can go to higher ground. The remaining 41 stories would provide 2,500 square meters of workspace per floor. An additional area would be cordoned off for IBC use. This would come in the form of 14,860 square meters of "compound space" adjacent to the Olympic Stadium and enclosed by a security perimeter. Members of the press would work in a currently standing facility. The MPC would be situated inside an existing portion of the Javitz Center and would yield 40,900 square meters of workspace. Most of the infrastructure needed is already in place. No permanent works would be required for the MPC. There would be two main areas available to the journalists in the facility. It would consume two 18,600 square meter floors as well as an additional penthouse of 3,700 square meters available for accredited press. Transportation for media members has been planned to expedite their daily journeys. An exclusive media bus system utilizing the Olympic Priority Lanes would serve the IBC/MPC, venues, hotels, as well as airports to provide convenience for members of the media.

HOTEL CAPACITY

Local organizers state that Madrid and its surrounding vicinity accept an average of 6 million tourists annually. Currently there are in the neighborhood of 68,000 rooms available in the Madrid metro area in the form of hotels, boarding houses, hostels, tourist apartments, and other types of accommodation. Current construction of three-, four-, and five-star hotels will see that number increase by 5,000 by the year 2006. By 2012, the total is expected to jump to 100,000 rooms of which 70,000 would be part of three-, four-, and five-star accommodations. The majority of these hotels would be located inside a 10 km radius of central Madrid thereby reducing commute times for visitors and spectators. Based on figures from 2003, the average nightly room rate for a five-star hotel in Madrid was $214.30, a four-star room was $94.54, and a three-star hotel would run you

\$83.20. Madrid's Hotel Association has ensured the IOC that it would undertake responsible and reasonable practices in setting rates during the Games. For the sailing venue at Palma de Mallorca there are currently almost 22,000 rooms available within a 10 km radius of the venue.

As recommended by the IOC, Madrid organizers would avoid the building of a "Media Village" by citing the fact that so many rooms would be available to journalists in central Madrid, near the Olympic Park, and adjacent to the International Media Center. Media outlets would receive a subsidized rate from the major national hotel operators. The OCOG would do its part to ensure that journalists would be located in accommodations nearest their venue of coverage. For cities other than Madrid, in the case of the sailing and soccer venues throughout Spain, a similar hotel offer would be in place for media members. All of the hotels that would be made available to the media community would have designated transport service to the airport, competition venues, and the International Media Center. These hotels would also be manned with information booths specifically serving media professionals.

The Moscow OCOG reports that there are currently over 33,500 hotel rooms available in Moscow. This number is expected to jump to approximately 61,000 rooms by 2012. About 38% of the existing three-, four-, and five-star rooms are situated within 10 km of central Moscow that would leave them close to the majority of the 2012 Games venues. The Moscow City Council has authorized the construction of 230 new hotels, all three-star or higher, by 2010. In data provided by the OCOG, the average nightly price as of July 2003 for a five-star room was $300, with a four-star suite costing $200, and a three-star accommodation running $50.

The accommodations for members of the accredited media would come in the form of a dedicated Media Village, to be constructed on 20 hectares of land within walking distance of the IBC and MPC and across the river from the Olympic Village. Travel times to most of the venues and center city would not exceed 15-20 minutes. The 17,000-room housing would be privately financed and would become private residential property following the Games.

According to the Paris OCOG, Paris and the Ile-de-France region receive the most number of tourists in the world annually and in 2002 welcomed some 44.6 million visitors. In a 50 km radius around center city Paris, over

2,300 hotels offer almost 140,000 rooms currently. Of those, over 55% are concentrated in the interior of Paris and 80% are located within a 10 km radius of the city's center. Organizers cite the constant upgrading of accommodations due to the heavy tourism volume for the addition of over 7,000 rooms in the last 3 years. Located 15 minutes outside Paris, the city of Lille can provide greater than 5,000 rooms nightly. In terms of other venue cities throughout France, Lyon has a hotel capacity of 10,600 rooms, Nantes provides 4,800 rooms, Marseilles is not far behind with around 4,700, La Rochelle has 3,600, and the town of Lens has over 500 rooms available. The OCOG reports that the average nightly rate for a five-star room is $330, for a four-star room is $120, and for a three-star hotel is $100.

With its vast hotel capacity, Paris organizers feel a media village would not be required to be constructed.

The London OCOG reports that the city welcomes 11.5 million visitors annually. There are over 70,000 rooms of three-, four-, and five-star quality situated within 10 km of central London. There are plans to add another 20,000 hotel rooms by 2012. Of these, 4,000 are currently under construction and 16,000 have received building permission. There are also over 6,500 rooms available in the form of hostels and residence halls throughout the city. The media would be offered exclusive hotels in the Bloomsbury area that would leave them 7 minutes via public transport from the Olympic Park. According the OCOG, the average nightly rate in London would be $428 for a five-star room, $232 for a four-star room, and $134 for a three-star room.

There would be no Media Village as the organizers feel that there is adequate hotel infrastructure to meet these demands.

It was estimated by the OCOG that over 40 million visitors came to New York in 2004. In a 10 km radius of Midtown Manhattan, there are, according to organizers, approximately 73,500 rooms provided by 261 hotels. The OCOG reports that there are 144 hotels providing close to 48,700 hotel rooms in Midtown Manhattan alone just minutes from where the Olympic Stadium would be. The organizers estimate a total of approximately 115,300 rooms in the New York City metropolitan area. As of 2003, as reported by the OCOG, the average nightly rate for a five-star room was $283, a four-star room would cost $260, and a three-star room would run $179. Within 10 km of Midtown Manhattan an additional 14,000 guest rooms are due to be constructed by 2012. Between 10 km and 50 km of Midtown, 12,000 rooms would be introduced by 2012.

No Media Village would be constructed, as exclusive hotels would be set aside for media use within minutes from the Olympic Stadium.

INFRASTRUCTURE OF TRANSPORT

Madrid organizers claim that, from a transport perspective, they are capable of welcoming the Olympic Community today with no problems with the road and public transport systems that are already established. Around 95% of the transport infrastructure that would apply to the Games has either been constructed or will be constructed regardless of Madrid winning the 2012 bid. The organizers are banking on the August holiday period in Spain along with the city's four ring roads to allow for hassle free traffic conditions. The city offers close to 100,000 public parking spaces and approximately 15,000 additional parking spaces throughout its many suburban train stations. One lane in each direction would be reserved for Olympic transport along the each of the ring roads. Madrid's subway system consists of 12 lines, a branch line, and mostly air-conditioned trains.

By 2007 there will be additional stations constructed throughout the Olympic Ring allowing access to all of the Madrid competition venue sites by subway or suburban rail. Madrid's road system spans a 50 km radius of the city center and boasts over 3,200 km of roads. In the vicinity of the city there are 7 motorways and 14 highways with the construction of 6 additional motorways to be complete by 2010. Two suburban train stations, one in the Olympic Park and another in the South Park of the Manzanares River, are also on the way. The Ministry of Public Works has approved a plan to utilize the AVE high-speed train to link Madrid with the cities of Alicante, Barcelona, and Málaga who would also be hosting Olympic competitions. This connection already exists between Madrid and Córdoba. Currently there is one flight every hour from Madrid's Barajas Airport to Palma de Mallorca's Son Sant Joan Airport with the sailing venue situated ten minutes from Palma's airport.

Barajas Airport would serve as the major port of entry for the 2012 Olympics. It currently accepts approximately 34 million passengers annually and is connected to 150 destinations worldwide. Current plans will double the airport's capacity and air traffic capability by 2005. The airport is located 12 km from central Madrid and the dedicated Olympic transport system would allow commuting to the Olympic Village in 5 minutes. Satellite baggage check-in services at the Nuevos Ministerios and Campo de Las Naciones subway station in the IFEMA fair grounds already available serve to increase convenience for travelers. Madrid has also implemented a noise monitoring system called SIRMA to check the level of overhead plane noise to protect the surrounding area and its plant life from environmental problems. Along with the directly linked subway and public bus service, there are also the A-10 and R-2 motorways and the N-II highway, which can be accessed from the city's 4 ring roads. Two new motorways were scheduled for completion in 2004 that link the airport to the city via the north/south and east/west artery roads currently under construction.

Two other regional airports, Torrejon Airport which is adjacent to Barajas and would be used for private flights as well as Cuatro Vientos Airport located southwest of the city and would accommodate light air traffic including helicopters etc., would also be available for use on the Madrid project and during the Olympic Games.

Madrid is responsible for carrying out the largest extension to a subway network in the world by adding 55.8 km of new track to give the city the second largest subway system in Europe. Further expansion is planned which will add 159 km of more tracks to the network over the next several years. The city is also developing all-in-one transport centers by combining subway, train, and bus stations as well as flight check-in services at certain transportation locations to increase efficiency for travelers.

The Madrid OCOG also aims to offer the world an Olympic Games without cars. They believe this can be achieved due to the dense concentration of the venues along with the vast public transport network. During the Games, the athletes and officials would be transported on exclusive "Olympic lanes" on the roads, media members would be within 30 minutes of each venue by public transport from their official hotels, and spectators would be able to travel to 21 competitions by public transport alone. The travel distances to all sporting venues excluding rowing, canoe/kayak, sailing, and selected soccer preliminaries would be less than 20 km and, therefore the organizers conclude, less than 20 minutes.

The Moscow OCOG states that all of the venues proposed for 2012 are located near a major road or public transport stop. The public transport system in Moscow is comprised of a series of buses, trolleys, trams, intercity rail lines, route taxis as well as the Metro or subway. The

Moscow Metro possesses 265 stations and carries between 6 and 8 million passengers daily. Currently there are 3 ring roads around the city with a fourth recently approved by the City Government to be completed by 2009. On these motorways and local radial roads, organizers plan to implement dedicated lanes for Olympic traffic.

Currently, the Moscow River is used mainly for tourism and recreational purposes. In the event of the city winning the bid, travel by ferry would be ramped up to help relieve stress on other transport systems.

Moscow's historic railway infrastructure is well established, with 9 stations serving domestic and international travel. In addition to these options, organizers are also planning to offer coach buses, minibuses, limousines, and helicopters as transport alternatives. The City of Moscow plans to limit freight transportation during the Games, implement dedicated Olympic road lanes and routes, and provide vehicular escort for select athletes and officials.

Most of the venues would be located between 5 and 20 minutes by road from the Olympic Village. The athletes would receive full coach bus transport to and from the venues. Members of the Olympic delegation would be provided cars and minibuses as needed. There would also be media shuttles to and from venues as well as serving the MPC and IBC. The general public would be able to use the variety of public transport or taxi options available in the city.

Moscow would be able to utilize three international airports and one domestic airport for the Games. The primary international airport that would serve the Games is Vnukovo, which is located about 30 minutes southwest of central Moscow. This airport is currently under construction to add 29 more gates that would increase its passenger capacity from 1100 to 2800 travelers per hour. Service carrying people from the airport to the city would come in the form of two motorways, the public transport network, and a high-speed rail line darting straight into the center of Moscow scheduled to be operational by 2011. Vnukovo was chosen as the main airport for Olympic purposes because of its location in relation to central Moscow and the fact that, owned by the City of Moscow, it could be most easily adapted to meet the needs of the Games. Shremetyevo International Airport, situated about 30 minutes north of Moscow, would be able to handle 6,600 travelers per hour by 2010, and have a high-speed rail line similar to Vnukovo by 2010 as well, in addition to the existing connection to the city via motorway and public transport. Located approximately 50 minutes south of central Moscow is the Domodedovo International Airport, capable of processing 2600 passengers per hour by 2010, and currently linked with Moscow via motorway and a dedicated railway branch line. Bykovo is a domestic airport that can be used for national or security air traffic.

Paris and its vicinity are served by a ring road going 4 lanes in both directions around the city. The region is home to a 576 km network of roads with multiple expansion and construction projects currently underway. Paris and the Ile-de-France region have 6 large-scale railway stations linking it to the rest of Europe. The subway or Paris Metro is a system composed of a suburban railway network, a regional express network (RER), a metropolitan railway network, as well as numerous tram routes. The Metro and RER combine to offer stops at over 700 stations throughout the vicinity. The city also offers public buses as an alternative means of transport whose 1,300 routes serve some 27,000 stops. The venues in cities outside of Paris would be accessible via high-speed train (TGV) as well as domestic flights from Paris. All of the current and proposed venues are accessible via public transport.

The public transport network and infrastructure is due to be upgraded and enhanced by 2012. The Northern Cluster would see the creation of the Evangile Station on the RER's E line along with an additional tramway line, the Paris-Tramway des Marechaux Est. The Saint-Denis Epinay Villetaneuse tramway's termination point would be extended from the Stade de France out to the Evangile station, thereby adequately serving the southern end of this cluster, Plaine Saint-Denis, as well as providing new transport to facilitate urban development in the future. For the Western Cluster, a temporary Metro station has been planned for the Longchamp Bagatelle (equestrian) venue. During the Olympics, the current Boulevards des Marechaux bus network would be temporarily expanded. Working plans have the currently under construction Tramway des Marechaux Sud being extended to the Porte d'Auteuil which is the main access center for the Western Cluster. Following the Games, this improvement would offer easier public access to the large Parisian park, Bois de Boulogne. Along the Seine River and Saint-Denis canal, ferries would be able to provide transport throughout the city.

In addition to motorways, the Vaires-sur-Marne (rowing/canoe/kayak) and Saint-Quentin-en-Yvelines (non-road cycling) would be linked to the nearest RER stations via dedicated bus shuttles. An express shuttle from the

DeGaulle airport to the center of town would be available for travelers.

Technologically, Paris plans to equip all train carriages and buses with onboard computerized information systems giving passengers real time updates on schedules, wait times, and delays.

According to organizers, traffic rates have been falling since 1997 as more people utilize the expanding public transport system. As of 2004, public transport provided for 63.6% in Paris and 29.4% in the Ile-de-France of all motorized journeys. By 2012, that share is expected to increase to 66% for Paris and 30% for the Ile-de-France region. The proposed timing of the Games would be when traffic levels are 15% below normal due to summer holidays.

To serve all of the transport needs, including advance study and extrapolation of data, Paris has formed the 2012 Strategic Transport Plan (STP), a dedicated committee to oversee safety, efficiency, reliability, and punctuality issues concerning the transport infrastructure. The Olympic Transport Organization (OTO) would be created approximately 3 years before the Olympics and would govern the Games transport process. There would also be dedicated road lanes for the Olympic Family as well as prespecified express routes to ensure punctual transport for athletes and officials. Members of the media would have dedicated shuttles to and from their relevant facilities. Paris has also proposed free 24-hour transport and park and ride access to spectators holding tickets.

Parking in and around the venues would be reserved for accredited Olympic vehicles only. Spectators arriving by car or coach would be provided with easily accessible park and ride facilities short distances away from their destination venue.

The primary airport for the Olympic and Paralympic Games would be Roissy Charles DeGaulle International Airport, which serves 48 million passengers annually. Located 35 km from Paris, it is linked to the city via the A1 and A3 motorways, RER express rail, and direct bus routes. It is one of the few airports in the world to have direct high-speed train service, via its TGV station in Terminal 2, to other major cities throughout France and Europe. Other airports that are available include Orly International (20 km from Paris and linked via bus and a proposed tram connection) and Le Bourget (16 km from Paris and linked via bus) to be used for dignitaries and security operations.

London possesses the world's busiest international airport and one of the world's largest rail and subway

(The Underground) systems. The OCOG reports that 12 million journeys are made on a daily basis using London's public transport system. During the August period of the Games, travel demand would be 20% lower, enough to accommodate the 5% increase usually seen during Olympic use. The Olympic Family would have 240 km of designated road lanes to provide convenience and shorter commutes. The Olympic Park would be served by 10 rail lines able to shuttle 240,000 travelers per hour. A special temporary high-speed train would be run courtesy of the Channel Tunnel Rail Link providing service between St. Pancras station in central London to the Olympic Park in 7 minutes.

In the event of London winning the hosting rights, an Olympic Transport Authority would be created by the UK Government to handle all transport related tasks. The government has also approved $30 billion in transport infrastructure upgrades by 2012. This plan includes the extension of the Docklands Light Railway in east London (also serving the London City Airport), extension of the East London Metro, as well as renovations on all London Underground stations. There would also be the addition of new stations, enhancement of the bus system, and upgrading of major roads including the A13.

The primary international airport serving the 2012 Games would be Heathrow, with its current passenger processing capacity of 64 million annually. The dedicated Heathrow Express rail link carries travelers the 20 km distance to London in a time of 15 minutes and is available to passengers every 15 minutes as well. Travelers also have the options of using The Underground, taxis, and local public transport to reach other locations throughout the city. Heathrow is currently implementing a $10 billion construction program that will add a fifth terminal by 2008 and increase the passenger capacity by an additional 20 million annually as well as providing new links between the airport and the city via Heathrow Express and Underground.

Stansted Airport, accommodating 19 million passengers annually, stands 35 km from London and has the Stansted Express rail line, which carries passengers directly to east London. It would play a role in passenger as well as cargo traffic during the Games. The Gatwick and Luton Airports are situated within 30 minutes from central London via direct high-speed rail links. These 2 hubs combine to accommodate 40 million passengers annually. The London City Airport processes about 1.6 million passengers annually. It is linked to the Olympic Park area by public buses and will be connected to the Park by the Docklands Light Railway Extension by 2006. The Channel Tunnel Rail Link would provide direct services from northern Europe to Stratford. The soccer venues across the UK as well as the sailing venue of Weymouth all have local airports to accommodate travelers coming from London and beyond.

The existing transport infrastructure in New York City moves over 10 million people daily on 2600 km of motorways, 1269 km of subway and suburban rail lines, and an increasing system of ferry routes. Over 15 major bridges and tunnels link the highways and parkways in and around the city. Adding to the security, only 3 of the venues, all outside New York City, would allow for spectator parking and even these would require boarding of shuttles for transport to the venue itself.

According to the OCOG, New York City's regional public transport system is responsible for close to 9 million passenger trips every weekday. The system is comprised of the largest subway network in the United States, 3 suburban rail services, local and regional buses, light rail, ferries, and inter-city rail.

The city's subway system, run by the Metropolitan Transit Authority (MTA), transports an estimated 4.5 million travelers every weekday along 1,100 km of track and linking 490 stations. Some 2.4 million people travel by bus in the city every day using 244 local and suburban routes throughout the region. The MTA operates over 4,500 buses in total. The city's largest bus terminal funnels some 7,200 buses, with destinations inside and outside the city, daily. Between Jersey City in New Jersey and Manhattan the PATH rail service carries 180,000 passengers every weekday, which may offer visitors alternate options outside the city. The New York metro area boasts the 3 largest suburban rail services in the United States and includes a system of 25 branch lines that reach over 100 km outside of Manhattan. The system is supported by 2 main terminals in Midtown Manhattan, a handful of regional terminals, and hundreds of local stations throughout the vicinity. Over 750,000 travelers are transported by suburban rail every day in the New York and surrounding area.

The growing ferry network around the city performs an estimated 100,000 passenger trips every weekday, which makes it the largest ferry operation in the country. Two blocks from what would be the Olympic Square Cluster is Penn Station, the most active rail station in the nation, with inter-city and high-speed rail links to major cities throughout America.

The OCOG offers that 21 of the 28 subway routes within New York City would provide service to at least one Olympic venue. Upon completion of the suburban rail link to the Meadowlands in New Jersey, all of the rail lines would serve Olympic venues. Numerous park and ride facilities exist throughout the region, offering alternatives to the use of private cars closer to the venues.

Approximately 20% of the Unites States population lives within a day trip of New York City by car or train. The AirTran train system provides convenient links from the area's airports to central public transport hubs.

Major transport upgrade programs currently underway include the $500 million renovation of Penn Station, a $6.3 billion commuter rail connection at Grand Central Terminal, and a $1.8 billion extension of the city's Number 7 subway line to the far west side of Manhattan.

Operating 24 hours a day, the New York metropolitan area's 3 major airports, JFK (located 38 minutes from the IBC/MPC and 28 minutes from the Olympic Village), Newark Liberty International (located 31 minutes from the IBC/MPC and 40 minutes from the Olympic Village), and LaGuardia (located 30 minutes from the IBC/MPC and 20 minutes from the Olympic Village) serve a combined 83.5 million passengers annually. JFK's AirTran monorail system links all of its terminals to the New York City subway system and the Long Island Railroad suburban rail network. Newark's AirTran connects all of its terminals with NJ Transit suburban rail and Amtrak intercity rail, which can be taken to New York. La Guardia airport, to be used to handle domestic flights, is linked to the city via bus, and all three airports have ample private coach, limousine, and taxi services available to reach just about any destination in the vicinity.

As previously mentioned, the Olympic Family would have the Olympic Priority Lanes available for expedited travel times.

CALENDAR AND GENERAL AREA CONDITIONS

The Madrid OCOG has determined that it is best to host the Games from the 10th of August to the 26th of August 2012. These dates were decided on a number of factors.

In studying meteorological data from 1993 to 2002, Spain's National Meteorology Institute provided organizers with data showing that this two-week period is optimal for hosting a sporting event such as the Olympics due to the region's mild to warm temperatures, limited rainfall, and reduced humidity (39%) at midday compared to the morning (61%). Temperatures generally range from 18 to 31 degrees Celsius and rainfall during this time occurs, on average, 2 days during the selected period. Madrid can also rely on its many parks, with their plant life, lakes, and ponds to help cool the city during summer. Palma de

Mallorca experiences a Mediterranean climate with mild temperatures and moderate to high winds on the seas to be used for the sailing competition.

In data covering 1998 to 2002 provided to the OCOG by the Environmental branch of the Municipality of Madrid, it was found that the least amount of urban waste (about 90,000 tons) was generated in August as opposed to the high month of October when 130,000 tons of waste was created.

The Madrid Transportation Consortium has informed organizers that the least road traffic and the lowest number of public transport journeys (around 55 million) take place in August compared to the most amounts of journeys (close to 100 million) in October.

The OCOG also learned from the National Statistics Institute that, in data collected from 1993 to 2002, hotel occupancy in Madrid was at its lowest in the month of August.

There are school and university holidays during this time that would free up the city's youth to participate in volunteer programs and experience the Games. Also, the major European professional sports leagues would not have started their seasons making both athletes as well as fan interest available for the Olympics.

The Paralympic Games would take place between the 12th of September and the 23rd September taking advantage of the climate, transport, and urban waste production benefits before the month of October when these factors are less than ideal for staging such an event.

The OCOG estimates that the city population of Madrid would be over 3.2 million by 2012 while the population of the entire Madrid metropolitan area is estimated to be over 5.8 million in that Olympic year.

The dates selected by the Moscow OCOG for hosting the Games are the 14th to the 29th of July 2012, with the Paralympics taking place from the 11th to the 22nd August 2012. Based on meteorological data over the past century, the selected dates have experienced an average of 18 to 25 degrees Celsius with low chance of rain, an average 65% humidity at midday, and mild winds. By 2012, Moscow's population is expected to be around 9.9 million people.

The Paris Games would take place from the 20th to the 5th of August 2012. These dates take into account the traditional local holiday period which would allow for volunteer availability, decreased stresses on the traffic and transport systems, and availability of local ticket buyers. This period also follows the July 14th national holiday making more local hotel rooms available. The Games would take place after annual large scale sporting events such as Wimbledon and the Tour de France and before the start of the European soccer season. The local population for Paris in 2012 is expected to be around 2.1 million and in the Ile-de-France region it is estimated to be 11.5 million in the Olympic year. The average temperature during these two weeks is between 19 and 26 degrees Celsius between 9 a.m. and 6 p.m. with the average humidity during this time being 55%. In viewing data from 1994 to 2002 the average number of days with rainfall during this period is 4 days. The average temperatures during these dates for La Rochelle range from 22 to 25 degrees Celsius.

The Paralympic Games would end on the first Sunday in September before the start of the French school year and resumption of normal business in the region following summer break.

The London OCOG has determined that the Olympics there would take place from the 27th of July to the 12th of August 2005 while the Paralympic Games would take place from the 31st of August to the 11th of September 2012. Due to the school holiday period, transportation demands are expected to be lower locally and the vacated rooms of university students can be used as extra housing space. The expected population by 2012 is estimated by the OCOG to be over 2.8 million in inner London and over 7 million in the London metropolitan area. During this period, organizers report that the average temperature in the London East Lea Valley at 3 pm is 22.7 degrees Celsius, the average humidity is 54%, and average rainfall occurs for 16.2 days during this period.

The OCOG in New York has chosen to host the Olympic Games from the 27th of July to the 12th of August 2012 and the Paralympic Games would take place from the 29th of August to the 9th of September 2012. No other major events would occur in the city to conflict with the Games during this period. The organizers report that the number of weekday bus and subway riders decreases during this time sufficient to allow for accommodation of the expected 500,000 daily visitors for the Games. Over the past 30 years the daily 3 p.m. temperature in New York has averaged 28 degrees Celcius. Minimal precipitation (an average of 4.29 cm of rain over the last 10 years) has been historically observed during this time of year.

In 2012 the population of New York City is expected to be around 8.6 million while the population projection for the city's metropolitan area is placed at 23 million people.

EXPERIENCE

Over the last ten years, Madrid and Spain have staged 25 world championships in Olympic sports or disciplines and 24 European championships in Olympic sports or disciplines. Four qualifying tournaments for Athens 2004 were held in Madrid and three world championships are scheduled for Madrid in 2005.

Moscow has a strong history of local sporting participation, having over 170 youth sport schools right in the city. The city itself has over 2,500 gyms, 150 swimming pools, 26 ice rinks, 60 shooting centers, and almost 3,500 sports fields to go along with almost 3,000 local sporting events taking place annually. The city has also hosted, in addition to the 1980 Summer Olympics, over 100 International and European championships.

The organizers point to France's large volunteer availability, the French sporting culture/history, as well as ample international hosting experience as advantages for having the ability to successfully host the 2012 Games. Over the past decade, Paris has hosted 10 major International and European Championships including the annual French Open and Tour de France events as well as the 1998 FIFA World Cup.

In addition to the annual London marathon, the British Capital has hosted 9 International Championships since 1996. In 2002, Manchester was the site for the Commonwealth Games in which 3,679 athletes from 72 nations competed in front of over 900,000 fans. London is also home to the annual Wimbledon Tennis Championships as well as numerous international soccer matches throughout the year. In 2006, Weymouth-Portland will host the World Junior Sailing Championships while Eton/Dorney will hold the World Rowing Championships.

New York annually hosts well-known events such as the US Open, New York City Marathon, and the Millrose Games. Since 2000 the city has hosted 24 world-class championship events. Giants Stadium in New Jersey hosted large-scale soccer events since it was a host venue for the Men's World Cup in 1994 and the Women's World Cup in

1999. Throughout the course of these events volunteers have played major roles and provided much needed enthusiasm event after event.

SECURITY

The main responsibility of providing security for the Games in Madrid lies in the hands of the Ministry of the Interior, which oversees operations in the areas of security and emergency management services. There would also be an Olympic Security Select Committee to provide the nuts and bolts planning, coordination, and execution of the security plan. This Committee would have reporting to them the National Police, Civil Guard, Intelligence Services, Municipal Police of Madrid, the Traffic Authority, Army, Air Force, Navy, local police, fire departments, emergency medical services, and any private security resources chosen to take part in the operation. There would be a central control center from which the security operation would be managed. Inside the venues there would be substantial presence of Federal Government forces. Public transport would also be heavily monitored for potential threats. The OCOG believes that the dense concentration of venues is an advantage to securing the Games and would provide security forces with a smaller and more compact region to focus their efforts.

The Ministry for Internal Affairs of the Russian Federation would undertake the security of the Moscow Games. The Ministry is responsible for personal security, prevention and suppression of crime, maintaining public order, as well as other law enforcement duties. The Ministry for Internal Affairs also oversees the Federal Security Service, the Civil Defense and Emergency Ministry, as well as the Defense Ministry. In 2012, these forces would be deployed throughout competition and non-competition venues as well as non-Olympic areas throughout the region. The total security personnel involved in these operations would hover near 50,000. A significant amount of pre-Olympic work involving the Russian Federation intelligence agencies as well as Interpol is planned if Moscow is selected to host the 2012 Games.

French security is the responsibility of the State, while in Paris, the Prefect of Police under the authority of the Minister of the Interior, Internal Security, and local laws are the responsible parties. For the Olympics, security agencies would have over 56,000 police and fire personnel as well as 2,000 volunteer emergency staff available. The security group would also include national reserve forces. In the Paris vicinity the Prefect of Police has command over all agents involved in the security and emergency services including police departments, support/logistics administrations, and emergency services. The Prefect also holds authority over the public transport police and mobile force units. Overall the Prefect has command over seven departments in the region concerning security, law enforcement, and emergency services. An area headquarters has been established to coordinate all security related activities.

The UK Government would be the primary responsible party for providing security in London during the Games. A Government strategy group, spearheaded by the Home Office, would report to the Cabinet Office to ensure proper planning and resources are in place for the job. The Metropolitan Police Service (MPS) of London would coordinate the safety operations. The MPS served on the seven nation Olympic Security Advisory Group for the 2004 Athens Olympic and Paralympic Games. The MPS would utilize a single central command structure reporting to the Government group and incorporating the fire and ambulance services, intelligence agencies, local authorities, and private security staff. There would be an Olympic Security Command Center as well as satellite control installations at all Olympic venues.

The New York City Police Department (NYPD) would have full operating responsibility for security during the Games in New York. The United States Secret Service would provide the primary Federal coordination. These two bodies would work with local, state, federal, and international law enforcement agencies to formulate and execute security operations for the Olympics. The NYPD can call upon its existing relationship with the United Nations and the resultant interaction with nearly every international security agency in the world to aid their efforts. The NYPD's 36,000 members would be mobilized in conjunction with the Federal Bureau of Investigation, U.S. Coast Guard, the Port Authority of New York and New Jersey, the Nassau County Police Department, the New Jersey State Police, and the New York State Police. The City's Office of Emergency Management already has its own center for emergency, transit, and medical response agencies throughout the region.

Best of luck to all of the cities for this and any future bids.

See you in 2012!

Printed in the United States
71508LV00001B/32

9 781420 862270